GOVERNMENT PROCEDURES AND OPERATIONS

INTERNATIONAL REGULATORY COOPERATION

ACTIVITIES AND ANALYSES

GOVERNMENT PROCEDURES AND OPERATIONS

Additional books in this series can be found on Nova's website under the Series tab.

Additional e-books in this series can be found on Nova's website under the e-book tab.

GOVERNMENT PROCEDURES AND OPERATIONS

INTERNATIONAL REGULATORY COOPERATION

ACTIVITIES AND ANALYSES

LENORE LYNCH

EDITOR

New York

For permission to use material from this book please contact us:
Telephone 631-231-7269; Fax 631-231-8175
Web Site: http://www.novapublishers.com

Additional color graphics may be available in the e-book version of this book.

Library of Congress Cataloging-in-Publication Data

ISBN: 978-1-63117-276-2

Published by Nova Science Publishers, Inc. † New York

CONTENTS

PREFACE

Trade has increased as a share of the economy for several years, but U.S. companies can face difficulties competing in foreign markets when countries apply different regulatory requirements to address similar health, safety, or other issues. GAO was asked to examine what U.S. agencies are doing to engage in international regulatory cooperation. This book provides an overview of U.S. regulatory agencies' international cooperation activities; examines ways that U.S. agencies incorporate outcomes from international regulatory cooperation activities and consider competitiveness during rulemaking; and examines factors identified by U.S. agencies and stakeholders that act as facilitators or barriers to international regulatory cooperation.

Chapter 1 – Report of the United States Government Accountability Office on International Regulatory Cooperation: Agency Efforts Could Benefit from Increased Collaboration and Interagency Guidance, dated August 2013.

Chapter 2 – Report of a Congressional Research Service Publication, on Transatlantic Regulatory Cooperation: Background and Analysis, dated December 22, 2011.

Chapter 3 – Executive Order submitted by the White House, dated May 1, 2012.

In: International Regulatory Cooperation
Editor: Lenore Lynch
ISBN: 978-1-63117-276-2

Chapter 1

INTERNATIONAL REGULATORY COOPERATION: AGENCY EFFORTS COULD BENEFIT FROM INCREASED COLLABORATION AND INTERAGENCY GUIDANCE*

United States Government Accountability Office

WHY GAO DID THIS STUDY

Trade has increased as a share of the economy for several years, but U.S. companies can face difficulties competing in foreign markets when countries apply different regulatory requirements to address similar health, safety, or other issues. GAO was asked to examine what U.S. agencies are doing to engage in international regulatory cooperation. This report (1) provides an overview of U.S. regulatory agencies' international cooperation activities; (2) examines ways that U.S. agencies incorporate outcomes from international regulatory cooperation activities and consider competitiveness during rulemaking; and (3) examines factors identified by U.S. agencies and stakeholders that act as facilitators or barriers to international regulatory cooperation. GAO analyzed documents and interviewed officials from seven

* This is an edited, reformatted and augmented version of the United States Government Accountability Office Publication, GAO-13-588, dated August 2013.

U.S. agencies that regulate products traded internationally and four U.S. agencies with government-wide roles and responsibilities. GAO also interviewed officials from 11 organizations representing business and consumer advocacy perspectives that reported or publicly commented on international regulatory cooperation. The scope of this study is not intended to be a complete catalog of agencies' activities and is not generalizable to all entities that have interests in this area.

WHAT GAO RECOMMENDS

GAO recommends the RWG include in forthcoming guidance on Executive Order 13609 tools to enhance collaboration, such as mechanisms to facilitate staff level dialogues. The Office of Management and Budget (OMB) did not have comments on the recommendation.

WHAT GAO FOUND

All seven U.S. regulatory agencies that GAO contacted reported engaging in a range of international regulatory cooperation activities to fulfill their missions. These activities include the United States and its trading partners developing and using international standards, recognizing each other's regulations as equivalent, and sharing scientific data. U.S. agency officials GAO interviewed said they cooperate with foreign counterparts because many products they regulate originate overseas and because they may gain efficiencies—for example, by sharing resources or avoiding duplicative work. Cooperation can address both existing and avoid future regulatory differences. Officials also explained how cooperative efforts enhance public health and safety, facilitate trade, and support competitiveness of U.S. businesses. Several U.S. interagency processes require or enable interagency collaboration on international cooperation activities. The Regulatory Working Group (RWG), chaired by OMB and the Trade Policy Staff Committee (TPSC) are forums that have different responsibilities related to the regulatory and trade aspects of international regulatory cooperation. U.S. regulatory agency officials said the current processes could benefit from better information sharing among agencies on the implementation of international cooperation activities and lessons learned. Without enhancements to current forums, opportunities to share practices and improve outcomes could be missed. Executive Order 13609, issued in May 2012, tasked the RWG with enhancing coordination and issuing guidance on international regulatory cooperation, which the RWG is developing. Nonfederal stakeholders GAO interviewed reported challenges to providing input on U.S. agencies' international regulatory cooperation activities, in particular that they are not always aware of many of these activities and participation can be resource intensive.

Officials GAO interviewed said the outcomes from international regulatory cooperation inform all phases of the rulemaking process, from helping an agency decide whether to regulate to implementing and enforcing regulations. U.S. agencies are not required to conduct a separate analysis on the competitiveness impacts on U.S. businesses when developing regulations. However, five of the seven U.S. agencies told GAO they do consider competitiveness. Officials we interviewed also pointed out that any analysis of impacts may not rise to the level of inclusion in the rulemaking record. In addition, U.S. agencies' use of international standards in regulations can lower costs for U.S. businesses and reduce barriers to trade. Officials from all of the U.S. agencies GAO interviewed said they consider international standards during rulemaking partly in response to requirements in trade agreements, U.S. statutes, and executive orders.

Officials from all of the U.S. agencies GAO interviewed identified seven key factors that affect the success of international regulatory cooperation activities: (1) dedicated resources, (2) established processes, (3) high-level leadership, (4) scientific and technical exchanges, (5) stakeholder involvement, (6) statutory authority, and (7) early and ongoing coordination. When present, these factors can facilitate U.S. agencies' efforts, but they can also act as barriers when absent. GAO found that these factors also reflect the seven key features for implementing collaborative mechanisms previously identified in its September 2012 report on interagency collaboration.

ABBREVIATIONS

(Q)SARs	Quantitative Structure-Activity Relationships
4E	Efficient Electrical End-Use Equipment
AMS	Agricultural Marketing Service
APA	Administrative Procedure Act
APEC	Asia-Pacific Economic Cooperation
APHIS	Animal and Plant Health Inspection Service

Commerce	Department of Commerce
CPSC	Consumer Product Safety Commission
DOE	Department of Energy
DOJ	Department of Justice
DOT	Department of Transportation
EMA	European Medicines Agency
EPA	Environmental Protection Agency
EU	European Union
FAS	Foreign Agricultural Service
FDA	Food and Drug Administration
FSIS	Food Safety and Inspection Service
FSMA	Food Safety Modernization Act
FTA	Free Trade Agreement
FTC	Federal Trade Commission
GDP	Gross Domestic Product
HC	Health Canada
HHS	Department of Health and Human Services
ICN	International Competition Network
IEA	International Energy Agency
ISO	International Organization for Standardization
ITA	International Trade Administration
NAFTA	North American Free Trade Agreement
NHTSA	National Highway Traffic Safety Administration
NIST	National Institute of Standards and Technology
NOP	National Organic Program
OAR	Office of Air and Radiation
OCSPP	Office of Chemical Safety and Pollution Prevention
OECD	Organisation for Economic Co-operation and Development
OIE	World Organization for Animal Health
OIRA	Office of Information and Regulatory Affairs
OMB	Office of Management and Budget
PAI	Pilot Alignment Initiative
PHMSA	Pipeline and Hazardous Materials Safety Administration
RCC	U.S.-Canada Regulatory Cooperation Council
RWG	Regulatory Working Group
SPS	Sanitary and Phytosanitary

SPS Agreement	WTO Agreement on the Application of Sanitary and Phytosanitary Measures
State	Department of State
TBT	Technical Barriers to Trade
TBT Agreement	WTO Agreement on Technical Barriers to Trade
TDG Subcommittee	Transport of Dangerous Goods Subcommittee
TPSC	Trade Policy Staff Committee
UN	United Nations
Unified Agenda	Unified Agenda of Federal Regulatory and Deregulatory Actions
USAID	United States Agency for International Development
USDA	United States Department of Agriculture
USTR	Office of the United States Trade Representative
WHO	World Health Organization
WP.29	World Forum for Harmonization of Vehicle Regulations
WTO	World Trade Organization

August 1, 2013

The Honorable Darrell E. Issa
Chairman
Committee on Oversight and Government Reform
House of Representatives

Dear Mr. Chairman:

U.S. exports and imports grew from 22.8 percent of gross domestic product (GDP) in 2002 to 31.4 percent of GDP in 2012, or a total of $4.9 trillion. Doubling U.S. exports by 2014 is a goal of the President's National Export Initiative.[1] Nonetheless, U.S. companies can find it difficult to compete in foreign markets when countries have different requirements for addressing similar health, safety, or other regulatory issues. International regulatory cooperation—agencies' engagement with foreign counterparts on issues related to their regulatory missions, such as international standards development, scientific collaboration, and information sharing—can help lower costs for businesses, increase U.S. exports, and further economic growth and job creation.[2] International regulatory cooperation can also have other benefits, including increasing the safety and quality of other countries' exports to the United States, thus helping to protect U.S. consumers. Some of our recent reports have shown that U.S. regulatory agencies have been struggling to adequately protect the public in the face of rising imports and increasingly complex supply chains.[3] For example, in September 2009, we reported that the Food and Drug Administration (FDA) needed to address gaps in enforcement and collaboration domestically and abroad to enhance the oversight of food imports.[4]

In May 2012, the President issued Executive Order 13609 on promoting international regulatory cooperation to provide high-level support and direction for U.S. agencies' international regulatory cooperation efforts. The executive order directed agencies to consider addressing unnecessary differences in existing regulations and describes processes to help avoid regulatory divergence in the future. Recent reports show that nonfederal stakeholders have mixed views regarding international regulatory cooperation. Some industry stakeholders are generally supportive of international regulatory cooperation efforts, especially in the context of reducing unnecessary barriers to trade,[5] while some consumer advocacy stakeholders expressed concerns that efforts to align U.S. regulations with trading partners could lower the protection of safety and health in U.S. regulations.

In this context, you asked us to examine what federal agencies are doing to engage in international regulatory cooperation. This report (1) provides an overview of regulatory agencies' international cooperation activities; (2) examines ways that agencies incorporate outcomes from international regulatory cooperation activities and consider competitiveness during rulemaking; and (3) examines factors identified by agencies and nonfederal stakeholders that act as facilitators or barriers to international regulatory cooperation and to considering competitiveness. For the purposes of this report, competitiveness refers to the ability of U.S. firms to sell into international markets.

To identify the U.S. regulatory agencies with a significant number of regulations related to international trade, we analyzed the 2010 and 2011 Unified Agenda of Federal Regulatory and Deregulatory Actions (Unified Agenda),[6] as well as data from the 2011 World Trade Organization (WTO) Technical Barriers to Trade (TBT) Information Management System. We applied criteria to select agencies that regulate products that are traded internationally and assure the inclusion of some independent regulatory agencies in our review. We analyzed documents and interviewed officials from seven U.S. regulatory agencies out of 60 U.S. agencies that are included in the Unified Agenda, including the Department of Energy (DOE), the

Department of Health and Human Services' (HHS) FDA, the Department of Transportation (DOT), the Environmental Protection Agency (EPA), the United States Department of Agriculture (USDA), the Consumer Product Safety Commission (CPSC), and the Federal Trade Commission (FTC). We selected these agencies because they regulate products that are traded internationally, such as medical devices, chemicals, toys, automobiles, and food. These views are not generalizable to all U.S. agencies. We reviewed documents and interviewed officials from the four agencies with government-wide regulatory and international coordination roles and responsibilities: the Office of Management and Budget (OMB), the Office of the United States Trade Representative (USTR), the Department of Commerce (Commerce), and the Department of State (State).[7] To obtain a broader set of perspectives, including those of participants from outside government agencies, we interviewed officials from 11 academic and stakeholder organizations representing business and consumer advocacy perspectives, such as the U.S. Chamber of Commerce and Public Citizen. We selected these organizations based on published views on international regulatory cooperation and recommendations from agencies in our study. These views are not generalizable, but provided insights. Using criteria based on our September 2012 report on interagency collaborative efforts, we also compared agencies' documents and testimonial evidence about their international regulatory cooperation activities to the seven key features that we found agencies should consider when implementing collaborative mechanisms.[8]

We tested the reliability of the databases used to help select agencies to include in this review by reviewing related documentation, interviewing knowledgeable agency officials, and tracing a sample of entries to source documents. We concluded that the data were sufficiently reliable for the purposes of this report. Throughout this report, we use specific, selected examples to illustrate general agency processes and practices. The scope of our inquiry is neither a complete catalog of international regulatory activities nor generalizable to all individuals who have interests in international regulatory cooperation and global competitiveness. Appendix I provides a more detailed description of our objectives, scope, and methodology.

We conducted this performance audit from March 2012 to August 2013, in accordance with generally accepted government auditing standards. Those standards require that we plan and perform the audit to obtain sufficient, appropriate evidence to provide a reasonable basis for our findings and conclusions based on our audit objectives. We believe that the evidence obtained provides a reasonable basis for our findings and conclusions based on our audit objectives.

BACKGROUND

U.S. Agency Roles and Responsibilities

U.S. agencies have different responsibilities related to international regulatory cooperation. For example, Commerce, State, USTR, OMB, and USDA have government-wide responsibilities. Their roles and responsibilities are determined primarily through statutes and executive orders. U.S. treaty obligations also influence their activities, as shown in table 1. To some extent these agencies bring structure and direction to activities that are in practice pursued in a decentralized manner by multiple agency participants.

U.S. regulatory agencies have varying missions, such as protecting public health or safety, and engage in multiple activities to fulfill their missions. Statutes establish agencies' missions and establish the scope and limits of each agency's authority. Agencies often implement their statutory missions by developing, issuing, and enforcing regulations. Agencies may also need to comply with multiple procedural and analytical requirements during the rulemaking process that precedes the issuance of regulations, including participation in interagency review and coordination processes summarized in table 1.

Table 1. Government-wide Roles and Responsibilities Related to International Regulatory Cooperation

Agency	Roles and Responsibilities
Department of Commerce (Commerce)	The role of Commerce's International Trade Administration (ITA) in international regulatory cooperation is generally to coordinate with industry to obtain its input on U.S. producers' concerns about global competitiveness and market access. ITA also has a role in some international regulatory cooperation initiatives, such as regulatory cooperation councils and has responsibility for monitoring compliance with nonagricultural international trade agreements to which the United States is a party. Commerce's National Institute of Standards and Technology (NIST) is responsible for notifying the World Trade Organization (WTO) of proposed regulations that could have trade impacts and serving as the U.S. national enquiry

Agency	Roles and Responsibilities
	point for the WTO Agreement on Technical Barriers to Trade (TBT Agreement). Per the National Technology Transfer and Advancement Act, NIST is also responsible for coordinating federal, state, and local technical standards and conformity assessment activities with the same activities of the private sector. The goal is to eliminate unnecessary duplication and complexity in the development and promulgation of conformity assessment requirements and measures.
Department of State (State)	The Secretary of State is responsible, on behalf of the President, for ensuring that all proposed international agreements of the United States are fully consistent with U.S. foreign policy objectives. According to State, no agency of the U.S. government may conclude an international agreement, whether entered into in the name of the U.S. government or in the name of the agency, without prior consultation with the Secretary or his designee.
United States Trade Representative (USTR)	USTR leads U.S. trade policy and coordinates the efforts of U.S. agencies to reduce barriers to trade such as discriminatory foreign regulations. It also represents the United States in international trade forums such as the WTO, oversees U.S. implementation of trade agreements, and monitors compliance with trade commitments. To prevent regulation-related trade barriers, it has promoted adoption of good regulatory practice guides by international economic forums.
Office of Management and Budget (OMB)	OMB coordinates interagency review of significant rulemakings. OMB also plays a leadership role in government-wide international regulatory cooperation initiatives, such as regulatory cooperation councils. Under Executive Order 13609, the Regulatory Working Group (RWG), chaired by OMB's Office of Information and Regulatory Affairs (OIRA), provides a forum for international regulatory cooperation.
Department of Agriculture (USDA)	USDA is the national enquiry point for the WTO Agreement on the Application of Sanitary and Phytosanitary Measures (SPS Agreement), coordinates U.S. government comments on foreign SPS regulations, and notifies the WTO of U.S. regulations that may have trade impacts. USDA houses the U.S. government offices for coordination with Codex Alimentarius Commission, World Organization for Animal Health, and International Plant Protection Convention, the three international standard setting bodies referenced by the SPS Agreement.

Source: GAO analysis of agency documents.

Regulatory Context

Regulation is one of the principal tools that the U.S. federal government uses to implement public policy. Underlying federal regulatory actions is the long-standing rulemaking process established by the Administrative Procedure Act (APA).[9] This act establishes broadly applicable federal requirements for informal rulemaking, also known as notice and comment rulemaking.[10] At a high level, domestic rulemaking activities governed by the APA generally include four basic phases:

1. Consideration of regulatory action: The agency gathers information to determine (1) whether a rulemaking is needed and (2) the range of regulatory options.[11]
2. Development and issuance of proposed regulation: The agency drafts a proposed regulation, including the preamble (the portion of the regulation that informs the public of the supporting reasons and purpose of the regulation) and the language in the regulation. The agency also begins to address analytical and procedural requirements and engages in interagency coordination and OMB review, where required. After these are complete, the agency publishes the proposed regulation in the *Federal Register* and requests comments from the public.
3. Development and issuance of final regulation: The agency responds to public comments, completes analytical and procedural requirements, engages in interagency coordination and OMB review where required, and publishes the final regulation in the *Federal Register.*
4. Implementation of final regulation: The agency enforces compliance with the final regulation and monitors its performance.

Various executive orders and guidance establish agencies' processes that govern international regulatory cooperation activities. Executive Order 12866 established the basic principles and processes that help guide and coordinate regulatory actions by executive agencies (other than independent regulatory agencies).[12] Three components of the order are especially relevant to current regulatory cooperation efforts. First, the order established general principles for government regulation, including that agencies should assess the costs and benefits of available regulatory alternatives. Second, the order established centralized review and coordination of rulemaking, particularly by (1) requiring agencies to submit draft significant regulations to OMB's Office of

Information and Regulatory Affairs (OIRA) for interagency review before they are published[13] and (2) establishing the RWG to serve as a forum to assist agencies in identifying and analyzing important regulatory issues[14] Third, the order required agencies to compile and make public their regulatory agendas and plans, which include identifying the anticipated effects of forthcoming regulations. Executive Order 13563 reaffirmed the principles, structures, and definitions governing contemporary regulatory review that were established by Executive Order 12866.[15] Particularly relevant to this report, the order states that the regulatory system must promote competitiveness, and it also expanded expectations for agencies to retrospectively review their existing regulations.

OMB periodically issues guidance to executive agencies on implementing executive orders. One key example related to the regulatory review orders discussed above is OMB Circular A-4, issued in 2003. The circular provides OMB's guidance on the development of regulatory analysis as required under Executive Order 12866 and related authorities, defining good regulatory analysis and standardizing the way benefits and costs of federal regulatory actions are measured and reported. The circular includes a brief paragraph about considering the impacts of federal regulation on global markets and trade. In May 2011, USTR and OMB released a joint memorandum restating U.S. trade obligations and provided additional guidance to agencies on how to carry them out. In particular, the joint memorandum stressed the importance of agencies' attention to regulatory analysis requirements in prior executive orders and OMB Circular A-4, as well as avoiding unnecessary barriers to trade as specified in the Trade Agreements Act. The memo also encouraged agencies to engage in international collaboration activities.

Trade Context

Some U.S. international regulatory cooperation efforts occur within the context of trade policy and negotiations. Reducing foreign regulatory barriers to trade is a key U.S. trade objective. In support of this objective, international agreements and U.S. legislation enacting them encourage and guide agencies' participation in some international regulatory cooperation activities. For example, the Uruguay Round Agreements Act codifies the WTO Agreement on Technical Barriers to Trade (TBT Agreement) and the WTO Agreement on the Application of Sanitary and Phytosanitary Measures (SPS Agreement) and includes additional international regulatory cooperation responsibilities.[16] Several of the most salient obligations are briefly described below.[17]

- TBT Agreement:[18] For technical regulations, the TBT Agreement requires members to use international standards or the relevant parts of them as a basis for technical regulations where available and appropriate, and, in certain instances, notify the WTO of proposed regulations with possible trade impacts and consider comments received before finalizing those regulations. Further, the TBT Agreement states that regulations should be no more trade restrictive than needed to fulfill a legitimate objective.
- SPS Agreement:[19] For SPS measures (including measures to protect animal or plant life from pests, diseases, or disease-causing organisms as well as to protect human or animal life), the SPS Agreement requires members to base their measures on existing international standards, or where the measure results in a higher level of protection, allows members to maintain or introduce their own standard if there is a scientific justification. Members are also required to ensure that their regulations are applied only to the extent necessary to protect human, animal, or plant life or health. Members are to notify the WTO at an early stage in the rulemaking if a proposed regulation differs from an international standard and may have a significant trade impact on other members, in order to receive comments for consideration.
- Free Trade Agreements (FTA): According to USTR, FTAs, such as the U.S. Korea Free Trade Agreement, build on the disciplines of the TBT Agreement, by providing for greater transparency. Some U.S. FTAs also provide that interested parties and persons should be given opportunities to comment on proposed measures. According to Commerce officials, most of these bilateral trade agreements also provide for more timely notification mechanisms than multilateral mechanisms such as the TBT Agreement. Most of these bilateral trade agreements also provide for more timely notification mechanisms than multilateral mechanisms.

In addition to these finalized agreements, the United States has offered proposals in ongoing Trans-Pacific Partnership negotiations toward a trade agreement among 11 participating nations to promote transparency. More recently, on February 13, 2013, President Obama and European Union (EU) leaders announced their intention to launch negotiations on a Transatlantic

Trade and Investment Partnership. According to USTR, the goals of the partnership include reducing the cost of differences in regulation and standards by promoting greater compatibility, transparency, and cooperation.

U.S. Agencies Engage in Six Primary Categories of International Regulatory Cooperation Activities

All agencies in our study reported that they engage in a range of international regulatory cooperation activities. These activities include U.S. agencies and foreign counterparts sharing scientific data, developing and using the same international regulatory standards, and recognizing each other's regulations as equivalent. Cooperation can address both existing and avoid future regulatory differences. These activities generally fall into six broad categories, as shown in table 2 below. See appendix II for details on the illustrative examples.

International regulatory cooperation activities involve bilateral and multilateral governmental relationships and participation in third-party organizations, such as standards-setting bodies. For example, some agencies in our study participate in international organizations, such as the World Organization for Animal Health (OIE)[20] or the International Organization for Standardization (ISO).[21] International cooperation activities may be formal or informal, ranging from participation in international organizations established by international agreements to informal regulatory information sharing and dialogues. International regulatory cooperation activities may also occur on a government-wide basis and address multiple sectors. For example, the U.S.-Canada Regulatory Cooperation Council (RCC) is an effort to increase regulatory transparency and coordination between the two countries. Action plans exist in the areas of agriculture and food, transportation, health and personal care products and workplace chemicals, the environment, and cross-sectoral issues. Similarly, OMB, Commerce, and other federal agencies also participated in the Asia-Pacific Economic Cooperation (APEC) effort to share and promote good regulatory practices, such as transparency and centralized review of regulations, among APEC economies.

Table 2. Categories of International Regulatory Cooperation Activities by U.S. Agencies

Activity	Description	Illustrative examples
Information sharing and scientific collaboration	Agencies share information with their foreign counterparts on scientific data and regulatory approaches.	• Pesticide Tolerance Crop Grouping Revisions Program • Chemical Data Information Sharing • Consumer Product Safety Pilot Alignment Initiative
Development and use of international standards	Agencies participate in international standards setting bodies and incorporate international standards into rulemaking as appropriate.	• World Forum for the Harmonization of Vehicle Regulations • UN Subcommittee on the Transport of Dangerous Goods • International Competition Network
Equivalency agreements	The United States enters into an agreement with another country to recognize their regulations and deem them equivalent to those of the United States.	• National Organic Program Equivalency Agreements • Equivalency Determinations for the Import of Meat, Poultry, and Egg Products
Strengthening capacity of developing countries	Most agencies in our study provide technical assistance to developing countries. Agency officials said they work with countries to strengthen their regulatory systems, among other reasons, to improve the safety of products imported into the U.S.	• Food and Drug Administration • Federal Trade Commission • Animal and Plant Health Inspection Service
Work sharing with foreign counterparts	Agencies work with foreign counterparts on projects to share resources to implement regulations and avoid duplicating effort.	• Food and Drug Administration Coordination on Inspections • Animal and Plant Health Inspection Service Joint Animal Health Site Visits to Third Countries

Activity	Description	Illustrative examples
Coordination on voluntary programs	Agencies cooperate with foreign counterparts on voluntary programs.	• Efficient End-use Electrical Equipment Implementing Agreement, Solid State Lighting Annex

Source: GAO analysis of agency documents and interviews.

Agencies Cooperate Internationally to Fulfill Regulatory Missions

Agency officials said they engage in international regulatory cooperation activities primarily because they are operating in an increasingly global environment and many products that agencies regulate originate overseas. For example, according to FDA's Global Engagement Report, the United States imports 80 percent of active pharmaceutical ingredients and imports of FDA-regulated products have grown dramatically in recent years. FDA reported that the agency engages in international cooperation activities to ensure products produced overseas are safe for U.S. consumers. Similarly, CPSC operates in an increasingly global environment. According to CPSC, the value of U.S. imports under CPSC's jurisdiction has skyrocketed in recent years, with imports from China more than quadrupling from $62.4 billion in 1997 to $301.0 billion in 2010. Moreover, in fiscal year 2012, 4 out of every 5 consumer product recalls or 345 of 439 recalls involved imported products, making imports a critical focus for CPSC.

Agencies also cooperate with foreign counterparts in an effort to gain efficiencies. For example, EPA participates in an initiative on pesticides through the Organisation for Economic Co-operation and Development (OECD) that has resulted in regulatory efficiencies. OECD also reported that, by accepting the same test results OECD-wide, unnecessary duplication of testing is avoided, thereby saving resources for industry and society as a whole.[22] A 2007 study for the OECD Working Group on Pesticides estimated resource savings of 33 to 40 percent as a result of joint review by three to five countries, compared with each country working alone. The study noted that the savings from reducing duplicative expert evaluation work significantly outweighed the marginal increase for project management, coordination, and travel.[23] These tools and approaches facilitate work sharing for regulators and help avoid costly, duplicative testing by ensuring that the data developed and submitted in one country can be used by other countries in reaching their regulatory decisions.[24]

Agencies' efforts to cooperate on regulatory programs through cooperative activities may also have the effect of facilitating trade and supporting the competitiveness of U.S. businesses. FDA officials said that international regulatory cooperation and harmonization has public health benefits, promotes regulatory efficiency, and both also have indirect competitiveness advantages for companies. FDA officials said that public health regulatory and competitiveness goals are often complementary: by upholding and enforcing scientifically valid standards, public health is protected and promoted at the same time that companies benefit from a level playing field that should make their products more competitive. Moreover, bringing a quality, safe, effective new drug to market faster yields health benefits for individuals because they have access to the drug sooner as well as trade benefits for industry, which has access to more markets.

In addition, U.S. agency officials said that when they participate in international standards development, an existing U.S. regulation or policy approach may be used as the basis for the international standard. When other countries adopt U.S. approaches to regulations, it can lower compliance costs and support competitiveness for U.S. businesses. For example, EPA's Office of Air and Radiation (OAR) officials said that OAR worked within the World Forum for Harmonization of Vehicle Regulations (WP.29) to urge the use of a U.S. regulation as the basis for a global regulation on test procedures for off-highway construction vehicle engines. OAR officials said U.S. manufacturers supported this effort because U.S. manufacturers sell equipment internationally, and complying with one set of regulations reduces their fixed costs.

2012 Executive Order Outlines New Processes for International Cooperation, but Agencies Could Benefit from Additional Collaboration

There are four interagency review processes routinely used to identify and review regulations that could have trade or competitiveness impacts and to encourage international regulatory cooperation.

- OMB officials said that a process for interagency coordination with OMB, USTR, State, and Commerce on regulations is the centralized regulatory review process under Executive Orders 12866 and 13563. USTR officials said they work with agencies as needed on regulatory issues that have an international impact prior to the interagency regulatory review process. However, the interagency review process ensures OMB, USTR, State, and Commerce another opportunity to provide input on any proposed significant regulation from agencies whether or not international impacts were raised earlier. Independent agencies are not required to participate in the interagency review process.

- The May 2012 Executive Order 13609 on promoting international regulatory cooperation establishes processes for agencies to report on efforts in this area. The order requires agencies that are required to submit a regulatory plan to report a summary of their international regulatory cooperation activities that are reasonably anticipated to lead to significant regulations in their regulatory plans. It also requires agencies to identify regulations with significant international impacts in the Unified Agenda, on Reginfo.gov,[25] and on Regulations.gov.[26]
- Generally, all U.S. federal agencies are required to consult with State before concluding international agreements.[27] Among other things, State is responsible for ensuring that any proposed international agreement is consistent with U.S. foreign policy. State officials said that the Secretary of State must be consulted on international regulatory cooperation issues involving the negotiation or signing of international agreements or arrangements.
- The Trade Agreements Act, as amended, requires U.S. agencies to coordinate in specified circumstances,[28] including with USTR on standards-related trade measures as part of their overall statutory responsibilities.

Current interagency review processes are designed to trigger reviews in certain instances, such as when agencies' international regulatory cooperation activities include significant regulations, international agreements, and trade mechanisms. Many of the international regulatory cooperation activities reported in our study would not trigger these processes, such as activities related to information sharing and scientific collaboration, capacity building, or the use of international standards in regulations that are not significant.

OMB and USTR also lead interagency forums on regulations and trade that have different responsibilities related to international regulatory cooperation. Executive Order 13609 assigns responsibilities to the Regulatory

Working Group (RWG), chaired by OMB's Administrator of OIRA, to serve as a forum to discuss, coordinate, and develop a common understanding among agencies of U.S. government priorities for international regulatory cooperation. According to OMB officials, the RWG provides a forum to foster greater cooperation and coordination of U.S. government strategies, including those for promoting regulatory transparency, sound regulatory practices, and U.S. regulatory approaches abroad. OMB officials also said that the RWG is developing guidance to implement the executive order. USTR chairs the policy-level Trade Policy Staff Committee (TPSC), which maintains U.S. interagency mechanisms for trade policy coordination among State, Commerce, the Department of Labor, USDA, and other appropriate agencies. The TPSC identifies and addresses foreign government trade measures among other duties. USTR officials said USTR coordinates with agencies on trade issues related to regulations at the working level through the TPSC subcommittees on technical barriers to trade and sanitary and phytosanitary barriers to trade. USTR explained that these subcommittees are involved in supporting international regulatory cooperation by anticipating and resolving potential regulatory conflicts that could impair trade. USTR officials also noted that at the TPSC subcommittee level, USTR coordinates with officials from regulatory agencies in preparing for participation in international cooperation activities, such as APEC meetings, as well as regulators' involvement in international standards development. Nevertheless, some agency officials reported that greater coordination between regulatory forums and trade forums could improve outcomes. USTR officials also said there is uncertainty about the implementation of Executive Order 13609 and how it will relate to USTR's trade responsibilities. According to OMB officials, one of the main objectives of Executive Order 13609 is to improve coordination of international regulatory cooperation. They anticipate that forthcoming guidance on Executive Order 13609 will address collaboration with the RWG and other interagency groups, particularly the TPSC.[29]

Beyond these forums for interagency coordination, regulatory agency officials we interviewed said the current processes could benefit from better information sharing among agencies on the implementation of international regulatory cooperation activities and lessons learned. We have previously found that it is important to ensure that the relevant participants have been included in the collaborative effort, including those with the knowledge, skills, and abilities to contribute to the outcomes of the collaborative effort.[30] The RWG and TPSC are designed for high- level, government-wide policy discussions, and participants in the RWG and TPSC are higher level management or policy officials who may be somewhat removed from the technical activities that underpin rulemaking.

Regulatory agency officials we interviewed pointed out that additional ways to facilitate exchanges about best practices and day-to-day implementation would be helpful. An agency official said that there may be a benefit to having an interagency dialogue, working group, or other forum through which officials can share information on challenges and successes in implementing international regulatory cooperation. For example, officials said EPA and FTC both have regulations related to labeling and there may be opportunities that could result from sharing information and best practices with international regulators. Agency officials we interviewed identified another example illustrating the potential benefits of staff-level exchanges and information sharing during a multiagency meeting on this report. The officials that we interviewed said it is challenging to measure the outcomes of international regulatory cooperation activities and there is a need for an appropriate metric to show the value of funds spent on these activities. EPA officials we interviewed stated that in one case they successfully quantified the benefits from work with OECD's Mutual Acceptance of Data program. According to EPA, the implementation of this decision has saved both governments of 34 member countries and industry nearly $225 million annually and also generated many nonquantifiable benefits, such as promoting animal welfare in chemical testing. Officials attending a GAO multiagency meeting said similar practices would be helpful to justify investments in international regulatory cooperation activities. Agency officials we interviewed said they found a multiagency meeting on this report useful in part because the meeting involved discussions of day-to- day implementation of these issues. Further, Commerce officials suggested that enhanced coordination among participants in these forums would also benefit from including existing interagency standards policy groups, such as the Interagency Committee on Standards Policy and the National Science and Technology Council's Subcommittee on Standards. Without some enhancements to the current forums for regulators and trade officials to collaborate, opportunities to share practices and improve safety and regulatory efficiencies and to reduce trade barriers could be missed. Agency officials said there is currently not a forum to meet this need.

Nonfederal Stakeholders Report Challenges to Providing Input into Agencies' International Regulatory Cooperation Activities

Although nonfederal stakeholder input into regulatory processes is important, the stakeholders we spoke with said it can be challenging for them to provide input into agencies' international regulatory cooperation activities because of the required resources and the difficulty of becoming aware of such activities. Congresses and Presidents have required agencies to comply with multiple procedural requirements in an effort to promote public participation in rulemaking, among other goals.[31] For formal international regulatory cooperation, such as standards setting, according to nonfederal stakeholders, they can directly observe international meetings and provide input in some cases. However, nonfederal stakeholders told us that high levels of resources are required to participate in international meetings, which can limit participation in practice. For informal international cooperation activities, nonfederal stakeholders said it is even more challenging to track and provide input into the agencies' activities because some activities described to us by regulatory agencies precede the decision to regulate and therefore may not be transparent to the public. While it is generally challenging for nonfederal stakeholders to provide input into U.S. agencies' international regulatory cooperation activities, it is particularly important that stakeholders at least have the opportunity to participate and advise agencies when those activities are anticipated to lead to the development of regulations. However, further complicating nonfederal stakeholders' efforts, there is no single source of public information on anticipated U.S. and foreign rulemakings with an international impact. For example, the Unified Agenda and OMB Regulatory Review Database both identify U.S. regulations that have an international impact. The Unified Agenda includes regulations under development or review, while the OMB Regulatory Review Database includes significant regulations submitted to OMB for review. In addition, the WTO maintains databases on certain member countries' proposed regulations related to technical barriers to trade and sanitary and phytosanitary measures—namely those self- identified as having potential trade impacts or involving divergence from international standards.

Agency officials we interviewed agreed that stakeholder involvement is important and nonfederal stakeholders are uniquely positioned to identity and call attention to unnecessary differences among U.S. regulations and those of its trading partners. Agencies and nonfederal stakeholders told us that the U.S.-Canada RCC has implemented practices to engage nonfederal stakeholders. For example, the 29 work plans that make up the RCC were developed in part from the response to a *Federal Register* request for public comments concerning regulatory cooperation activities that would help eliminate or reduce unnecessary regulatory divergences in North America that disrupt U.S. exports. Stakeholder outreach activities are also included in the work plans. OMB is also taking steps to increase the transparency of agencies' international regulatory cooperation activities and included new reporting requirements for agencies in Executive Order 13609. The order directs agencies that are required to submit a regulatory plan to include summaries of their international regulatory cooperation activities that are reasonably anticipated to lead to significant regulations.[32] An agency official also cautioned it may not be realistic for agencies to report all international regulatory cooperation activities as many are informal in nature.

AGENCIES CONSIDER INTERNATIONAL REGULATORY COOPERATION AND COMPETITIVENESS DURING RULEMAKING IN DIFFERENT WAYS

International Regulatory Cooperation Activities Inform Different Phases of Rulemaking

Agency officials we interviewed reported that the outcomes from international regulatory cooperation can inform all phases of the rulemaking process, from affecting an agency's decision whether or not to regulate in a particular area to implementing and enforcing regulations. According to an agency official, there is no bright line that separates international regulatory cooperation activities from regulatory programs. For example, U.S. agencies share scientific and technical information with their foreign counterparts, which can inform all stages of the rulemaking process. In addition, information sharing can help inform an agency's decision on whether or not to regulate a product. When countries have differences in regulations in a particular area, there are opportunities to coordinate on the science underlying regulatory decisions in a particular area. EPA Office of Chemical Safety and Pollution Prevention (OCSPP) officials said that for chemical safety regulations, countries are working within different statutory and regulatory frameworks and different levels of acceptance of risk that can make it difficult to reach full agreement on a regulatory approach. In such cases, sharing information with foreign counterparts can facilitate agreement on a common understanding of the issue or on underlying technical or scientific issues. According to officials that we interviewed, OCSPP also focuses on transparency and good regulatory practices, which lead to commonality between policies, work sharing on scientific reviews, and greater harmonization in the long term.

Some international regulatory cooperation activities, such as the development of international standards or practices, can inform and contribute to the development and issuance of a proposed regulation. Certain U.S. agencies reported that they coordinate with organizations that develop international standards and may use these standards when developing domestic regulations. For example, DOT's Pipeline and Hazardous Materials Safety Administration (PHMSA) participates in the United Nations (UN) Transport of Dangerous Goods (TDG) Subcommittee, which develops UN Model Regulations for the transportation of hazardous materials. In an effort to align with any changes to the UN Model Regulations, PHMSA considers these model regulations in a rulemaking every 2 years. As a result, related U.S. regulations are more closely aligned with trading partners and there are fewer country-unique regulations for businesses to comply with, which leads to improved safety results. According to PHMSA officials that we interviewed, when regulations are the same in different countries it enhances compliance and improves the efficiency of the transportation system by minimizing regulatory burdens and facilitating effective oversight. Similarly, Commerce officials pointed out that regulators often use common technical standards as the basis for regulation, which can reduce the burden on the regulated community.

Other international regulatory cooperation activities are related to the implementation of regulations, such as equivalency agreements that assure compliance with U.S. requirements and capacity building. For example, USDA's Agricultural Marketing Service (AMS) manages equivalency agreements for organic food labeling. The U.S. equivalence arrangement with the EU allows organic products certified in Europe or the United States to be sold as organic in either region. According to AMS officials, equivalency agreements result in expanded market access, fewer duplicative requirements, and lower certification costs for organic products. Previously, businesses that wanted to trade organic products had to obtain separate certifications for both the United States and EU, which meant a second set of fees, inspections, and paperwork. Agencies also engage in capacity building and provide technical assistance to countries to help foreign businesses comply with U.S. regulations when exporting to the United States. For example, FDA developed a comprehensive international food safety capacity-building plan in response to a requirement in the FDA Food Safety Modernization Act. The plan establishes a strategic framework for the FDA, describes an approach that is based on prioritizing risks to U.S. consumers, and focuses on addressing system weaknesses working with foreign government and industry counterparts and other stakeholders. Agencies also engage in work-sharing arrangements with their foreign counterparts to gain efficiencies in the implementation of regulatory programs. For example, under the United States-Canada Beyond the Border Initiative, USDA's Animal and Plant Health Inspection Service (APHIS) conducted a joint foot and mouth disease site visit in Colombia as part of the evaluation of Colombia's request to export fresh beef. Coordinated inspections allow agencies to leverage resources with their foreign counterparts to fulfill their regulatory responsibilities. OIRA also engages in activities to strengthen the capacity of developing countries in several contexts, including APEC and work with Brazil, Vietnam, and Morocco.

Some international regulatory cooperation activities that U.S. agencies shared with us are on products that are not regulated by U.S. agencies. Agencies do not issue regulations through programs where participation is voluntary but still may coordinate with foreign counterparts. For example, DOE is working with other countries through the Efficient Electrical End-use Equipment (4E) Implementing Agreement on efficiency and performance criteria and metrics, test methods, and qualified testing laboratories for new technology for solid state lighting. DOE officials said coordination on solid state lighting is important, because without a common agreement, it would be more difficult for products to enter the world market. Standardized labeling also helps customers understand the product they are buying and how its efficiency compares with other products.

While Executive Orders and Guidance Encourage U.S. Agencies to Consider Competitiveness Impacts during Rulemaking, There Is No Requirement to Conduct a Separate Analysis

For regulations deemed significant under Executive Orders 12866 and 13563, U.S. agencies are required to assess the costs and benefits, but there is no requirement for agencies to conduct a separate analysis on competitiveness impacts when developing regulations. Among the general principles of regulation under Executive Order 13563 is that the U.S. regulatory system should promote economic growth, innovation, competitiveness, and job creation. Moreover, according to executive orders on regulatory review, among the possible effects that agencies should consider are the significant adverse effects on the ability of U.S. companies to compete in domestic and foreign markets. Moreover, OMB Circular A-4's discussion on global competitiveness states: "The role of Federal regulation in facilitating U.S. participation in global markets should also be considered. Harmonization of U.S. and international rules may require a strong Federal regulatory role. Concerns that new U.S. rules could act as non-tariff barriers to imported goods should be evaluated carefully." Further, these executive orders and related guidance do not apply to independent agencies.[33] The concept of competitiveness is a general one, referring to the set of institutions, policies, and human and natural endowments that allow a country to remain productive.

Depending on the circumstances, the focus of analysis could vary. Here, in the context of international regulatory cooperation, improvements to competitiveness might arise from lowering the cost of a firm's compliance with other countries' standards or expanding access of U.S. products to foreign markets. However, documenting the effect of the removal of barriers on firm cost and sales presents challenges because data on individual firm performance may not be available and because the effect of the regulatory action may be difficult to isolate. Still, in some cases, it may be possible to describe effects in terms of magnitude and direction.

When agencies develop regulations related to international activities, officials from five of the seven agencies in our study told us that they consider competitiveness as needed. Officials from two agencies in our study provided examples of analysis of competitiveness impacts in the rulemaking record. Agency officials said competitiveness impacts for some rulemakings are likely to be indirect and may not rise to the level of inclusion in the rulemaking record. For example, according to officials, APHIS's regulations focus on preventing the introduction and spread of pests and diseases of livestock and plants. The officials explained it is difficult to point to any APHIS regulations that can be said to have a direct effect on the ability of U.S. businesses to compete in the marketplace. In another example, officials from DOT's PHMSA said their regulations related to pipeline safety are for pipelines within the United States. When included in the rulemaking record, competitiveness is likely to be a secondary or tertiary effect in rulemaking analysis. For example, according to OAR officials, most OAR rulemakings have few if any direct impacts on competitiveness. These impacts, if any, would likely be secondary or indirect. They said that competitiveness analysis, when appropriate, might examine whether increased production costs for a U.S. business may put it at a competitive disadvantage compared with a similar company in a different country that is not required to comply with a similar environmental regulation.

Some agency officials we interviewed said competitiveness impacts can be challenging to identify, difficult to quantify, and resource intensive to complete and that they do not have tools to consider competitiveness during rulemaking. According to DOT's National Highway and Traffic Safety Administration (NHTSA) officials, NHTSA has never addressed the competitiveness of U.S. businesses in any of its analyses. NHTSA does not have tools for analyzing the effects of its safety standards on the competitiveness of U.S. businesses. For at least 10 years, NHTSA and DOT's Volpe Center have attempted to create a consumer-marketing model to help estimate the impact of the fuel economy program on sales and have been unsuccessful to date.[34] They said that trying to determine the impact on competition of a relatively small safety standard, when NHTSA cannot do it for the enormous fuel economy standard, does not seem to be a good use of resources.

However, officials from one agency we interviewed said that competitiveness impacts are assumed to exist when they are aligning regulations with trading partners, but agencies do not do a separate analysis. For example, according to PHMSA officials, PHMSA's harmonization rulemakings are premised on the assumption that harmonized standards reduce costs for businesses and therefore reduce barriers to trade. Specific cost-benefit analysis, however, is generally associated with comparing the estimated costs of a regulation with the safety and efficiency benefits associated with a specific change and not directly associated with competitiveness of U.S. businesses. Further, the TBT Agreement explains that using international standards as the basis of a technical regulation adopted for a specified legitimate objective shall be rebuttably presumed to not create unnecessary obstacles to international trade.[35]

U.S. Agencies Report Considering International Standards during Rulemaking

Officials from all U.S. agencies said they consider international standards during rulemaking, which can help facilitate trade. For example, NHTSA considers other countries' standards and regulations when developing new regulations. The agency considers the research and test procedures that have already been developed internationally when considering how to develop Federal Motor Vehicle Safety Standards. Similarly, DOE officials said DOE's Appliance and Equipment Standards Program regularly adopts (in whole or part) product test procedures (or test standards) developed by a broad range of nongovernmental standards organizations, such as the American National Standards Institute, the Institute of Electrical and Electronics Engineers, ASTM International,[36] the Illuminating Engineering Society, and others. Many of these test standards are referenced in, or used as the basis for, standards developed by organizations, such as the International Electrotechnical Commission, ISO, or other international standards-setting organizations. Agencies may also consider approaches taken by other countries. For example, in the development of a crib safety regulation, CPSC staff reviewed requirements of existing voluntary and international standards related to cribs. The primary standards currently in effect are CPSC standards for full-size cribs, which reference the ASTM voluntary standard; a Canadian standard; a European standard; and an Australian and New Zealand standard. ASTM considered the existing international standards in the development of the current ASTM voluntary standard.

The TBT Agreement includes requirements to use international standards or their relevant parts as the basis for technical regulation where available and appropriate; to participate in international standards development, within the limits of their resources; and to avoid unnecessary obstacles to trade.[37] Similarly, under the National Technology Transfer and Advancement Act of 1995, agencies are required to use technical standards that are developed or adopted by voluntary consensus standards bodies unless they are inconsistent with applicable law or otherwise impracticable.[38] If using standards other than voluntary consensus standards, agencies are also required to provide an explanation to OMB. Further, Executive Order 13609 on promoting international regulatory cooperation includes a requirement that for significant regulations that the agency identifies as having significant international impacts, agencies consider, to the extent feasible, appropriate, and consistent with law, any regulatory approaches by a foreign government that the United States has agreed to consider under a regulatory cooperation council work plan. DOT, CPSC, FDA, and USDA have some additional agency-specific documents related to considering international standards during rulemaking.[39]

KEY FACTORS CAN POSITIVELY OR NEGATIVELY AFFECT THE OUTCOMES OF INTERNATIONAL REGULATORY COOPERATION ACTIVITIES

Agency officials that we interviewed identified seven factors that have the greatest impact on improving the effectiveness of international regulatory cooperation. Some of these factors can facilitate agencies' efforts if present in international regulatory cooperation activities while others can also act as a barrier when absent. In an environment of constrained budgets, agencies may not be able to address the factors equally, so it is particularly important for agencies to focus on the factors that facilitate their efforts. Therefore, as part of our evaluation, we ordered the factors in table 3 below based on discussions and written responses from agencies.

As another part of our evaluation of these factors, we found that they align with each of the key features important for agencies to consider when implementing collaborative mechanisms. In September 2012, we identified features that agencies could benefit from considering when implementing interagency collaborative mechanisms.[40] For example, we found that: (1) resources are a key feature because collaborative efforts can take time and resources in order to accomplish such activities as building trust among the participants, setting up the ground rules for the process, attending meetings, conducting project work, and monitoring and evaluating the results of work performed; (2) establishment of agreements in formal documents can strengthen an agency's commitment to working collaboratively; and (3) leadership is important to all collaborative efforts, but agencies have said that transitions within agencies or inconsistent leadership can weaken the effectiveness of any collaborative mechanism. We used those features as criteria to determine whether the seven main factors that agencies and stakeholders identified as affecting international regulatory cooperation reflected consideration of each of those issues. We applied these criteria by comparing agencies' characterizations of the seven key factors affecting international regulatory cooperation to the specific questions identified in our 2012 report for agencies to consider when implementing collaborative mechanisms. That comparison demonstrated that one or more of the seven key factors corresponded to each of the features of effective collaborative mechanisms.

Table 3. Key Factors Identified by Agencies that Affect International Regulatory Cooperation

Factor	Description
Dedicated resources	Agencies can develop relationships with foreign counterparts, monitor developments and attend meetings when resources for regulatory cooperation are made available.
Established processes	Documented processes such as forums, international procedures, and other international mechanisms can govern certain international cooperation activities.
High-level leadership	Leadership can set the direction, pace, and tone of agencies' international regulatory cooperation activities.
Scientific and technical exchanges	The sharing of scientific and technical information with foreign counterparts can support the enforcement of regulations through universal compliance requirements and testing but can also lay the groundwork for future coordination.
Stakeholder involvement	Nonfederal stakeholders' participation in regulatory cooperation can help identify opportunities, but the effectiveness of participants can depend on the needs of various nonfederal stakeholders.
Statutory authority	Statutory authority can encourage or restrict participation in certain international regulatory cooperation activities.
Early and ongoing coordination	Coordination prior to the promulgation of regulations can prevent the establishment of regulations with unnecessary differences, but international regulatory cooperation requires ongoing commitment to be most effective.

Source: GAO analysis of agency interviews.

Note: The factors are listed in order of the general priority expressed by agency officials in meetings with GAO.

Dedicated resources. Agencies in our study emphasized that international regulatory cooperation requires dedicated resources and long-term investments. Agency officials that we spoke with said that the initial stage of international regulatory cooperation is resource intensive because it includes developing relationships with foreign counterparts and addressing legal, policy, and technical differences. In our September 2012 report, we concluded that resources are a key feature to collaboration because it takes time and resources to build trust among participants, set up ground rules for the process, attend meetings, conduct project work, and monitor the results of the work.[41] These agency officials also said that once the initial resources have been invested, reoccurring cooperation after implementation of regulations may be less resource intensive to maintain through monitoring of developments in foreign countries and by directly participating in formal and informal meetings. USDA Foreign Agricultural Service (FAS) officials also pointed out that it can take a long time before payoffs or results from resources invested in international regulatory cooperation become apparent.

Agency officials that we interviewed also identified some challenges to securing and sustaining resources for international regulatory cooperation activities. For example, officials said that international cooperation may be viewed as too resource intensive to inform each individual regulatory activity. Officials also said that investment in international regulatory cooperation is viewed in some agencies as optional if it conflicts with other priorities and responsibilities when the same staff members are needed for other regulatory activities. One FAS official said that one of the greatest resource constraints is securing the availability of regulators in his department. Agency officials said that their foreign counterparts also face resource constraints that may affect their participation in two ways. First, resource constraints may limit their ability to participate in international regulatory cooperation activities. Second, such constraints may encourage foreign counterparts to leverage their limited resources with the United States and other partners when the issues line up with their own priorities.

Officials identified some opportunities for leveraging funds from other agencies to participate in international activities on an ad hoc basis. To encourage compliance with the TBT Agreement, U.S. law authorizes the United States Trade Representative and the Secretary concerned to make grants to and enter into contracts with any other federal agency to assist that agency in implementing programs and activities such as participating in international standards-related activities.[42] For instance, one industry official said that agencies are going to have fewer resources and therefore should be interested in leveraging their resources with other countries as early as possible. Agency officials confirmed that there are opportunities for them to leverage funds from United States Agency for International Development (USAID) and State to participate in international meetings. In addition, USTR officials said that their agency is able to leverage funds that are not available to other U.S. agencies and can match funds for regulators to meet with their foreign counterparts in an international setting, such as through APEC meetings. U.S. participation in international regulatory cooperation can be a multi-agency effort. However, officials from a different agency also cautioned that such funds tend to be limited to efforts that involve developing countries and expressed concern that they are unlikely to be used to support regulators' participation with the EU. With reductions to the federal budget, the money available to support regulatory cooperation may shrink.

Established processes. According to agency officials, having defined long-term processes and accountability mechanisms in place for working with foreign counterparts can facilitate international regulatory cooperation. Officials also said that such established processes can increase transparency for stakeholders and better enable input. Agencies said that defined processes developed through international agreements, including forums, international procedures, and other international mechanisms, are helpful. Agreements, such as the WTO SPS Agreement, require members to consider international standards during their process to develop regulations. The WTO SPS Agreement generally obligates members to base their regulations on sanitary or phytosanitary measures on international standards from Codex, OIE, or the International Plant Protection Convention unless they have scientific justification or have determined a different level of protection through a risk assessment. In our September 2012 report, we concluded that the establishment of agreements in formal documents can strengthen an agency's commitment to working collaboratively.[43] Similarly, officials from DOT's PHMSA said established processes for the UN TDG Subcommittee facilitate their cooperative efforts. The OECD also has established processes on chemicals in their rules. The binding nature of OECD rules ensures all countries abide by the requirements to accept data from other OECD members, which helps advance its international regulatory coordination efforts.

High-level leadership. Agency officials told us in our interviews that high-level leadership within an agency and leadership from outside the agency can facilitate international regulatory cooperation, but a perceived lack of high-level commitment or changing priorities can serve as barriers. One academic expert said that the only way that international regulatory cooperation will work is with high-level attention from the White House, OMB, USTR, and the State Department. In addition, OMB officials we interviewed said high-level support and leadership is essential to the success of international regulatory cooperation. They also stressed that regulatory agencies must have buy-in themselves, rather than be coerced into international regulatory cooperation by outside agencies. Similarly, Commerce's International Trade Administration (ITA) officials said that executive orders and presidential initiatives, such as Executive Order 13609, the U.S.-Canada RCC, the U.S.-Mexico High Level Regulatory Cooperation Council, APEC leaders' meetings, and the North American Leaders Summit, have increased visibility, encouraged action from the regulatory community, and prioritized events related to international regulatory cooperation. Agency officials said that commitment of resources is an indicator of top-level support. Agencies also said that active participation by agency leadership with foreign counterparts can expedite and facilitate progress at key points. FDA officials said that, in their experience, when the heads of agencies have an ongoing active relationship with their counterparts in foreign countries, international regulatory cooperation is more likely to produce results.

Agencies told us that it can be challenging when leadership priorities change, such as when a new administration establishes different priorities, because international regulatory cooperation activities are long- term efforts. Shifting political priorities can lead to short-term commitments that can make it difficult for agencies to see projects through to the end. Officials said that agencies need high-level commitment, but if it wanes agencies can be left part way into a long-term project. In our September 2012 report, we concluded that, given the importance of leadership to collaborative efforts, transitions and inconsistent leadership can weaken the effectiveness of any collaborative mechanism.[44]

Scientific and technical exchanges. Sharing scientific and technical information facilitates international regulatory cooperation and includes coordination on testing, enforcement, and compliance issues, but, as explained later, can also be restricted by statutory authority. The FTC provides technical assistance to other countries in developing their regulatory policies. When countries disagree on the appropriate policy or standards, they can sometimes find agreement on the underlying scientific and technical basis for regulations. According to FDA officials, the regulations for medical products are more science based, while those for food are more culture based, so FDA has more success with international coordination on medical products. Collaboration and sharing of data can lay the groundwork for future coordination. An independent advisory agency developed a report that stated that the mutual trust between regulators is an opportunity for work sharing because agencies do not have to duplicate tests or science which allows them to share their workload with foreign counterparts, move limited inspectors or transfer other resources to areas of greater need. However, some statutes may restrict scientific and technical exchanges because of limits on the disclosure of information with foreign counterparts which is further discussed within the section on statutory authority.

Stakeholder involvement. Agencies we interviewed identified coordination with nonfederal stakeholders, such as industry groups, academic experts, and consumer groups, as a facilitator of international regulatory cooperation. An FDA official said that nonfederal stakeholders may be uniquely positioned to identify unnecessary differences in regulations and standards between countries and help agencies prioritize which differences would be most meaningful to address from their perspective. For example, FTC officials said that in developing the work products of the International Competition Network (ICN) a significant number of business users and nongovernmental advisors bring attention to issues, provide outside perspectives, help produce work products, and encourage implementation, even though government agencies are the members that ultimately accept the work by consensus.

Some agency officials and nonfederal stakeholders reported challenges to stakeholder involvement. Regulatory cooperation can be more difficult to resolve when nonfederal stakeholders have conflicting viewpoints about regulations. For example, USDA officials said there can be challenges when consumer advocacy groups and business advocacy groups have different views that lead to lawsuits to prevent international regulatory alignment. USDA officials said that the support for a U.S.- Canada pilot project for meat inspection was divided between businesses that supported it and consumer groups that did not. In addition, one industry group found that some regulatory agencies were unwilling to actively engage foreign counterparts and U.S. industries to discuss U.S. regulatory requirements that are adopted by other countries. A different industry representative said that a regulatory agency he works with independently created a division dedicated to international telecom issues to work with foreign counterparts and developed a modular approval, which gives industry more flexibility and shortens the time for product approvals.

In addition, a consumer advocacy stakeholder said that it would be helpful to set government-wide policies and definitions through a notice and comment period. For example, federal agencies do not employ the same definition of “equivalency,” and it would be helpful if there was a specific government-wide policy that stated that the result of international regulatory cooperation cannot lower domestic standards.

Statutory authority. Agencies we interviewed said that statutory authority may facilitate or limit their international regulatory cooperation activities. For example, DOT PHMSA officials said that statutory authority may mandate agency participation in international standards organizations. An industry stakeholder said it would facilitate cooperation if the underlying statutory authorities of agencies clearly permitted them to engage in trade activities. However, when statutes are prescriptive regarding domestic or rulemaking requirements, they can limit agencies' ability to make changes to regulations that align with a foreign trading partner. For example, agency officials said that statutes mandating use of specific technologies can remove the flexibility to coordinate with foreign counterparts. EPA officials also said that, in many instances, the Clean Air Act requirements may limit the degree to which domestic regulations can be altered to accommodate or conform to foreign or international standards or approaches. Statutes that mandate completion of rulemakings within short time frames can also limit agencies' ability to engage in harmonization. For example, CPSC officials said it was challenging to work with other countries to reach consensus when CPSC had been mandated by the Consumer Product Safety Improvement Act of 2008 to issue a large number of regulations in a short time frame, which limited the amount of time they had to work with foreign counterparts.

Some agency statutes may limit disclosure of company-specific information with foreign counterparts. This can prevent U.S. agencies from sharing certain reports and scientific information with trusted foreign counterpart agencies. In a previous report, we stated that, although the addition of section 29(f) to the Consumer Product Safety Information Act was intended to encourage information sharing, CPSC expressed concern that restrictive language in this section hindered its ability to share information.[45] An official from EPA OCSPP said that an important first step to scientific and technical exchanges with foreign counterparts is removing existing legal, regulatory, or policy hurdles that limit or prohibit data sharing between governments. For example, NHTSA officials we interviewed said that they have many research, testing, and enforcement activities that include restrictions on the transfer of information, which has been a barrier to international regulatory cooperation. They said that when a company discovered defects in tires in Germany, the information was not immediately available in the United States to prevent injuries because of an information-sharing restriction. Agency officials also noted that, in addition to the removal of U.S. agency information-sharing restrictions, it is essential that the hurdles that exist in other countries also be removed.

Early and ongoing coordination. Early and ongoing coordination with foreign governments in emerging areas before regulations are in place may facilitate international regulatory cooperation. Agency officials we interviewed said early and ongoing efforts are important to maintain progress. OMB officials said it is easier to prevent unnecessary differences than remove existing differences in regulations. For example, CPSC attends multilateral forecasting sessions with other countries to engage foreign counterparts before the rulemaking and standards setting process begins. According to agency officials we interviewed, it is more efficient for CPSC to align and prevent different regulatory approaches with other jurisdictions before the U.S. notice and comment rulemaking process begins. In another example, State officials we interviewed said there is a need for international regulatory coordination to take place as early as possible, before too many regulations are established in each country. They said there are opportunities to avoid unnecessary differences in regulations for nanotechnology, which can be applied to many types of products. Currently, there are no entrenched regulatory systems that would hinder cooperation on developing new standards. Industry officials also said that it is important to coordinate on requirements early by reviewing countries' regulatory differences, because fundamental differences between countries may require changes on an issue-by-issue basis. They also urged early coordination because regulatory agencies in other countries are establishing standards when the manufacturing process has already been developed in the United States, which does not work well for them within today's markets. One academic representative we interviewed said it is much easier for agencies to coordinate with trading partners on new regulations than on existing regulations.

According to agency officials we spoke with, early and ongoing coordination with foreign counterparts also can identify issues that are not ready for international regulatory cooperation. It is important to coordinate early with their counterparts when there are differences between the openness of the United States' and other countries' rulemaking processes. Officials noted that, while other countries have the opportunity to comment whenever a U.S. regulation is proposed, U.S. agencies and nonfederal stakeholders may not have similar opportunities to comment on foreign regulations.

CONCLUSION

With trade expanding and regulatory challenges growing, in recent years the President and U.S. agencies have undertaken multiple initiatives to focus attention on the importance of international regulatory cooperation. While the executive order on promoting international regulatory cooperation focuses on reducing trade barriers by reducing unnecessary differences in regulations with U.S. trading partners, we found in our review that U.S. agencies carry out numerous and diverse international regulatory cooperation activities to improve the effectiveness of regulations, gain efficiencies, and avoid duplicating work. The examples agencies shared with us show that their efforts often achieve both trade and regulatory efficiency goals. Ultimately it is clear that international regulatory cooperation requires interagency coordination. No one U.S. agency has the expertise or processes to effectively conduct these activities. Not only must regulatory agencies collaborate with other U.S. agencies, but they need to effectively collaborate with their foreign counterparts and affected nonfederal stakeholders.

Overall coordination of international regulatory cooperation activities is now handled by discrete processes with somewhat different focuses. U.S. regulatory agencies focus primarily on their missions to protect public health and safety and the environment, while USTR and Commerce, among others, focus on trade. Therefore, it is important for the U.S. government to effectively coordinate these interagency activities. Our work at agencies engaged in regulatory cooperation efforts shows there are opportunities to augment existing guidance and mechanisms that could further promote and improve international regulatory outcomes. For example, U.S. regulatory agency officials emphasized the benefits of sharing information on lessons learned and best practices with their peers. However, they believe the current processes are designed for top- level collaboration and do not sufficiently address the day-to-day implementation of international regulatory cooperation.

U.S. agencies and nonfederal stakeholders also noted the importance of stakeholder input in the success of international regulatory cooperation. Yet it is challenging for stakeholders to stay apprised of agencies' activities and therefore provide input to agencies. Key next steps could focus on identifying tools to measure outcomes as well as to document savings from more efficient use of government resources. In an environment of constrained resources it is even more important for agencies to share knowledge on the effective implementation of international regulatory cooperation.

RECOMMENDATION FOR EXECUTIVE ACTION

To ensure that U.S. agencies have the necessary tools and guidance for effectively implementing international regulatory cooperation, we recommend that the Regulatory Working Group, as part of forthcoming guidance on implementing Executive Order 13609, take the following action:

- Establish one or more mechanisms, such as a forum or working group, to facilitate staff level collaboration on international regulatory cooperation issues and include independent regulatory agencies.

AGENCY COMMENTS AND OUR EVALUATION

We provided a draft of this report to Commerce, CPSC, DOE, DOT, EPA, FTC, HHS, OMB, State, USDA, and USTR for their review and comment. We received written comments on the draft report from DOE, and CPSC in which they agreed with the recommendation to the RWG. In an email received on July 30, 2013, the Deputy General Counsel, Office of Management and Budget, stated that OMB had no comments on the recommendation in this report. However, OMB provided technical comments which we incorporated as appropriate. Commerce, CPSC, DOE, FTC, HHS, State, USDA, and USTR also provided technical comments which we incorporated as appropriate.

Sincerely yours,

Michelle Sager
Director, Strategic Issues

APPENDIX I. OBJECTIVES, SCOPE, AND METHODOLOGY

Our objectives were to (1) provide an overview of regulatory agencies' international cooperation activities, (2) examine ways that agencies incorporate outcomes from international regulatory cooperation activities and consider competitiveness during rulemaking, and (3) examine factors identified by agencies and nonfederal stakeholders that act as facilitators or barriers to international regulatory cooperation and considering competitiveness. To address these objectives, we selected seven U.S. regulatory agencies out of 60 U.S. agencies that are included in the Unified Agenda of Federal Regulatory and Deregulatory Actions (Unified Agenda), that issued regulations with international impacts and four U.S. agencies with government-wide international coordination responsibilities. Based on several sources we identified likely regulatory agencies that issue regulations related to international trade. For example, we reviewed the 2010 and 2011 Unified Agenda and data from the 2011 World Trade Organization (WTO) Technical Barriers to Trade (TBT) Information Management System. We also reviewed all major regulations from 2011.[46] We categorized the regulations with an international impact into regulatory subject areas such as product safety, environmental, energy, transportation of products, food, medical devices, drugs, and aviation. The reason we categorized the regulations was to select groups of regulations that affect global trade in products. In addition, we excluded categories from our scope, such as taxation/taxes, patents, arms trade, international waters, and trade agreements. We also tested the databases used in agency selection by reviewing related documentation, interviewing knowledgeable agency officials, and tracing a sample of entries to source documents. We concluded the data were sufficiently reliable for the purposes of this report. We also considered recommendations from federal agency officials in selecting regulatory agencies. From these varied efforts, for our review we selected the Department of Energy (DOE), Food and Drug Administration (FDA), Department of Transportation (DOT),[47] Environmental Protection Agency (EPA),[48] and Department of Agriculture (USDA)[49] as well as two independent regulatory agencies including the Consumer Product Safety Commission (CPSC) and the Federal Trade Commission (FTC). These views are not generalizable to all U.S. agencies. Based on our background research and suggestions from federal agencies we selected four agencies with government-wide international coordination responsibilities: Office of Management and Budget (OMB), Office of the United States Trade Representative (USTR), Department of Commerce (Commerce), and

Department of State (State).[50] Furthermore, using criteria based on our September 2012 report on interagency collaborative efforts, we also compared agencies' documents and testimonial evidence about their international regulatory cooperation activities to the seven key features that we found agencies should consider when implementing collaborative mechanisms to corroborate the agencies' findings.[51]

To obtain viewpoints outside of government, we chose 11 U.S. nonfederal stakeholders which consisted of academics, organizations representing businesses, consumer advocacy groups, standards setting organizations and industry representatives, based on their recent reports or from comments they made on international regulatory cooperation. We originally selected one of each type of nonfederal stakeholder group based on published views on international regulatory cooperation and recommendations from agencies in our study but decided to add more nonfederal stakeholders to our selection criteria to represent a diverse range of members that represent business promotion, consumer advocacy perspectives and neutral parties. These views are not generalizable, but provided insights on international regulatory cooperation.

For federal agencies and nonfederal stakeholders chosen for this engagement, we conducted interviews and gathered documentation such as concrete examples, facilitators, barriers, goals, outcomes, and stakeholder involvement related to international regulatory cooperation activities, rulemaking and global competiveness. We used this documentary and testimonial evidence to identify government-wide and agency-specific requirements related to rulemaking outcomes for international regulatory cooperation and global competitiveness and determined how these selected agencies consider related issues. After analyzing our evidence for common themes and patterns, we developed a summary document of factors that are facilitators or barriers to international regulatory cooperation and held two meetings for agency officials to reflect upon the meaning of the factors, and confirm their importance. We summarized information gathered at these group meetings to better describe the agencies' perspectives. Throughout this report, we use specific, selected examples to illustrate agency processes and practices.

The scope of our inquiry was not comprehensive, generalizable, or designed to be a complete catalog of international regulatory activities. We conducted this performance audit from March 2012 to August 2013, in accordance with generally accepted government auditing standards. Those standards require that we plan and perform the audit to obtain sufficient, appropriate evidence to provide a reasonable basis for our findings and conclusions based on our audit objectives. We believe that the evidence obtained provides a reasonable basis for our findings and conclusions based on our audit objectives.

APPENDIX II. EXAMPLES OF INTERNATIONAL REGULATORY COOPERATION ACTIVITIES

Agencies provided us with examples of their international regulatory cooperation activities. The examples below illustrate the types of activities that agencies engage in to fulfill their regulatory missions and are not meant to be a comprehensive catalog of agency activities in this area.

Information Sharing and Scientific Collaboration

Agencies share information with their foreign counterparts on scientific data and regulatory approaches.

Pesticide Tolerance Crop Grouping Revisions Program

Agency: Environmental Protection Agency's (EPA) Office of Chemical Safety and Pollution Prevention (OCSPP)

Description: OCSPP shares information with the North American Free Trade Agreement (NAFTA) partners and the international organization Codex on its Pesticide Tolerance Crop Grouping Revisions Program. EPA regulates pesticides by setting limits on the amount of pesticides that remain in or on foods marketed in the United States under the Federal Food, Drug, and Cosmetic Act. The Pesticide Tolerance Crop Grouping Revisions Program enables the establishment of tolerances for a group of crops based on residue data for certain crops that are representative of the group. Representatives of a crop group or subgroup are those crops whose residue data can be used to establish a tolerance on the entire crop group or subgroup.

The project involves several interrelated multiyear efforts, including (1) one with NAFTA partners in Canada and Mexico to revise the existing crop groups in EPA's regulations (40 CFR 180.41) to add new crops and create new groups and subgroups; and (2) one in which NAFTA partners are working with international stakeholders to modify the Codex crop groups, to support global trade and the use of data extrapolation. Petitions to revise the NAFTA crop grouping regulations are developed by the International Crop Grouping Consulting Committee, a group of more than 180 crop, agrichemical, and regulatory experts representing more than 30 countries and organizations. NAFTA partners also are working cooperatively with international stakeholders to revise the Codex system of classification of foods and animal feeds and to revise the Codex crop groups. Involvement by NAFTA member countries in the Codex process should help standardize commodity terminology and crop groupings within the global context.

Outcomes: Approved revisions to crop group regulations are formalized in the United States through rulemaking. EPA is currently working on its fourth crop grouping proposed regulation. Crop groupings also facilitate international trade, including the market for pesticide products and the crops treated. Pesticides with established tolerances in the United States can be sold for use on crops grown in other countries that intend to import those crops to the United States. Crops imported in the United States with pesticide residues that do not have an established U.S. tolerance are subject to enforcement action.

Organisation for Economic Co-operation and Development (OECD) Chemical Safety

Agency: EPA's Office of Chemical Safety and Pollution Prevention (OCSPP)

Description: The United States has participated in the OECD Joint Meeting of the Chemicals Committee and Working Party on Chemicals, Pesticides and Biotechnology, an organization with over 30 member countries, for more than 30 years. Specific information sharing activities include:

- OECD eChem Portal: OCSPP shares information on industrial chemicals and various data systems. The OECD eChem Portal allows simultaneous searching of reports and datasets by chemical name and number and by chemical property. The portal provides direct links to collections of chemical hazard and risk information prepared for government chemical review programs at the national, regional, and international levels. The portal also provides, when available, classification results according to national/regional hazard classification schemes or to the Globally Harmonized System of Classification and Labeling of Chemicals.

- OECD (Quantitative) Structure-Activity Relationships [(Q)SARs] Toolbox: OCSPP's (Q)SARs are methods for estimating properties of a chemical from its molecular structure. The toolbox is a software application for governments, chemical industry, and other nonfederal stakeholders to fill gaps in (eco)toxicity data needed for assessing the hazards of chemicals.

Outcomes: According to EPA, these tools and approaches reduce compliance costs for nonfederal stakeholders, facilitate work sharing for regulators, and help avoid costly, duplicative testing by ensuring that the data developed and submitted in one country can be used by other countries in reaching their regulatory decisions. These activities do not directly result in rulemakings, but can inform rulemaking activities.

Pilot Alignment Initiative (PAI) on Consumer Product Safety

Agency: Consumer Product Safety Commission (CPSC)

Description: CPSC participates in an international pilot alignment initiative with staff from the central consumer product safety authorities of Australia, Canada, the European Union, and the United States. This ad hoc group is not aligned formally with any existing multilateral forum. The participants are to seek consensus positions on the hazards to children and their potential solutions for three products: corded window coverings, chair-top booster seats, and baby slings. The goal of this initiative is to bring about effective, aligned safety requirements for these products to reduce injuries and save lives. The consensus positions could be considered and developed for implementation in each jurisdiction, according to the jurisdiction's preferred model, whether through regulation or voluntary standards. Officials said that the consensus papers for baby slings and chair-top booster seats are in progress.

According to CPSC officials, the PAI jurisdictions worked for 18 months to reach consensus positions on corded window coverings, but the project fell short of CPSC's expectations. Officials said that the technical teams from five jurisdictions agreed in principle that "no exposed cords" was the best solution to the strangulation hazard, but the European Commission had already publicly expressed an opposing position regarding the elimination of cords.

CPSC officials said that when the PAI work began, the European Commission had already moved into policy development and soon thereafter issued a mandate to the European Committee on Standardization explicitly permitting safety devices to keep exposed cords out of reach of children. As a result, the consensus paper recognized "no exposed cords" as the best solution but did not call for their elimination as a consensus approach.

Outcomes: According to CPSC officials, the PAI can result in similar product safety requirements at a high level of safety among the jurisdictions participating in the initiative.

Development and Use of International Standards

Agencies participate in international standards-setting bodies and incorporate international standards into rulemaking as appropriate.

World Forum for the Harmonization of Vehicle Regulations (WP.29)

Agencies: Department of Transportation's (DOT) National Highway Traffic Safety Administration (NHTSA) and Environmental Protection Agency's (EPA) Office of Air and Radiation (OAR)

Description: WP.29 is a permanent working party created more than 50 years ago in the United Nations (UN) that administers three international agreements on motor vehicles: (1) the 1958 Agreement concerning the adoption of uniform technical prescriptions for wheeled vehicles, equipment, and parts which can be fitted and/or be used on wheeled vehicles and the conditions for reciprocal recognition of approvals granted on the basis of these prescriptions, (2) the 1997 Agreement concerning the adoption of uniform conditions for periodical technical inspections of wheeled vehicles and the reciprocal recognition of such inspections, and (3) the 1998 Agreement concerning the establishing of global technical regulations for wheeled vehicles, equipment, and parts which can be fitted and/or be used on wheeled vehicles. The WP.29 develops Global Technical Regulations that are used in member countries' regulations and works as a global forum allowing open discussions on motor vehicle regulations. NHTSA and OAR participate in the development of global technical regulations. Nongovernmental organizations may also participate in a consultative capacity in WP.29 or in its working groups.

Outcomes: NHTSA officials said WP.29 participation contributes to safety in the United States because NHTSA leverages research with other countries. Global Technical Regulations increase alignment between countries. As a result, manufacturers have fewer country-specific regulations to comply with when participating in foreign markets. NHTSA uses Global Technical Regulations in rulemaking. For example, NHTSA issued a final rule in August 2012 on motorcycle brake systems safety standards to add and update requirements and test procedures and to harmonize standards with a global technical regulation for motorcycle brakes.

OAR officials said that OAR participated in an effort that focused on test procedures for off-highway construction vehicle engines. According to officials, this effort was undertaken after the completion of a domestic regulation. U.S. manufacturers supported using U.S. regulation as the basis of the Global Technical Regulation because U.S. manufacturers sell equipment internationally, and complying with one set of regulations reduces their fixed costs. Over 5 years OAR successfully worked within the WP.29 to make the U.S. regulation the basis of the WP.29 Global Technical Regulations. As a result, it has become the de facto standard around the world.

UN Subcommittee on the Transport of Dangerous Goods (TDG Subcommittee)

Agency: Department of Transportation's (DOT) Pipeline and Hazardous Materials Safety Administration (PHMSA)

Description: PHMSA participates in the TDG Subcommittee, which, according to PHMSA, is facilitated by two treaties: the Chicago Convention on International Civil Aviation and the International Convention for the Safety of Life at Sea. Officials said the TDG Subcommittee was established because there was a need for international coordination on the transport of dangerous goods. Participants in the TDG Subcommittee include 29 countries with voting status and numerous countries and nongovernmental organizations with observer status. The TDG Subcommittee reviews proposals from voting member countries and observers in relation to amendments to the UN Model Regulations and issues relevant to its work program. PHMSA represents the

United States at these meetings and formulates U.S. positions based on feedback from U.S. industry, the public, and other government agencies. PHMSA ensures coordination on U.S. positions, taking into account the interests of the DOT administrations and other government agencies. PHMSA's staff provides the technical support and resources to ensure that the positions taken are sound and justified based on pertinent data, technical analyses, and safety rationales.

Outcomes: PHMSA considers the standards developed by the TDG Subcommittee in a rulemaking every 2 years in an effort to harmonize with international changes. For example, in January 2013, PHMSA issued a final regulation on harmonization with international standards for hazardous materials. PHMSA amended the Hazardous Materials Regulations to maintain alignment with international standards by incorporating amendments, including changes to proper shipping names, hazard classes, packing groups, special provisions, packaging authorizations, air transport quantity limitations, and vessel stowage requirements. The resulting cooperation leads to aligned regulations with trading partners, fewer differences in regulations businesses must comply with, and improved safety results (e.g., common labels for hazardous materials). Harmonization of international and domestic standards enhances compliance and improves the efficiency of the transportation system by minimizing regulatory burdens and facilitating oversight. International harmonization of hazardous materials regulations plays a significant role in enhancing safe transportation through improved regulatory consistency.

International Competition Network (ICN)

Agency: Federal Trade Commission (FTC)

Description: In October 2001, the FTC, Department of Justice (DOJ), and 13 other antitrust agencies founded the ICN to provide a venue for agencies that regulate competition issues worldwide to work on competition issues of mutual interest. The ICN has a broad membership—127 agencies from 111 jurisdictions, which includes most of the world's competition agencies. The ICN works exclusively on competition issues; develops consensual, nonbinding recommendations and reports to bring about procedural and substantive convergence; and provides a significant role for nongovernmental advisors from the business, legal, consumer, and academic communities, as well as experts from other international organizations. The ICN is organized into working groups composed of agencies and nongovernmental advisors. Current working groups address unilateral conduct, mergers, cartels, agency effectiveness, and competition advocacy. The FTC led the merger working group's work on notification and procedures, which developed a set of eight guiding principles and 13 recommended practices for merger notification and review.

Outcomes: A major accomplishment of the ICN is that numerous members adopted key aspects of ICN recommended practices, such as those concerning merger thresholds. According to FTC officials, the objective was to enhance the effectiveness of each jurisdiction's merger review practices and processes and promote procedural convergence, thereby reducing unnecessary private and public costs and burdens associated with merger review. FTC officials said FTC has not done any rulemaking to implement the ICN recommendations because the recommendations are consistent with U.S. approaches to merger notification and review processes.

Equivalency Agreements

In some cases, the United States may enter an agreement with another country to recognize other's regulations and deem them equivalent to those of the United States.

National Organic Program (NOP) Equivalency Agreements

Agency: United States (USDA) Agricultural Marketing Service (AMS)

Description: The AMS manages equivalency agreements for organic food labeling. For example, the United States has an equivalency arrangement with the European Union (EU), generally referred to as the Partnership, under which organic products certified in Europe or the United States may be sold as organic in either region. For retail products, labels or stickers must state the name of the U.S. or EU certifying agent and may use the USDA organic seal or the EU organic logo. Under the Partnership, according to USDA, the EU and the United States agreed to work on a series of technical cooperation initiatives to promote organic production and establish common practices for assessing and recognizing organics programs of third countries.

Outcomes: According to USDA officials, the EU-U.S. organic equivalency arrangement reduces the cost of certification for organic producers and handlers because producers and handlers only need to be certified under one standard (either USDA organic regulations or EU organic regulations) but can now access and sell in both markets. Another outcome is that considering the respective countries' standards as "equivalent" facilitates international trade of organic products. According to AMS officials, equivalency agreements will result in expanded market access; reduce duplicative requirements and lower certification costs for the trade in organic products; and decrease the burden of administration. The agreements are also expected to open new possibilities for trade. Previously, operations that wanted to trade organic products on both sides of the Atlantic had to obtain separate certifications to meet both standards, which meant a second set of fees, inspections, and paperwork. Additionally, in most cases, the Partnership will provide exporters the opportunity to serve both the U.S. and EU markets from a single inventory of organic products.

Equivalence Determinations for the Import of Meat, Poultry, and Egg Products

Agency: USDA Food Safety and Inspection Service (FSIS)

Description: Food safety equivalency evaluations are based on provisions in the Agreement on the Application of Sanitary and Phytosanitary Measures, which appears in the Final Act of the Uruguay Round of Multilateral Trade Negotiations, signed in Marrakech April 15, 1994. Under the agreement, World Trade Organization (WTO) member countries shall accord acceptance to the sanitary and phytosanitary measures of other countries (even if those measures differ from their own or from those used by other member countries trading in the same product) if the exporting country demonstrates to the importing country that its measures achieve the importer's appropriate level of sanitary and phytosanitary protection.

FSIS makes determinations of equivalence by evaluating whether foreign food regulatory systems meet the level of protection provided by the U.S. domestic system. FSIS evaluates foreign food regulatory systems for equivalence through document reviews, on-site audits, and port-of-entry re-inspection of products at the time of importation. FSIS regulations list 46 countries as eligible to export meat, 9 countries as eligible to export poultry, and 2 countries as eligible to export egg products to the United States.

Outcomes: According to FSIS officials, the equivalency determination program has several benefits. One benefit is that the equivalence process requires communication and participation by U.S. regulators with the regulators in the country seeking (or already having) equivalence, which usually leads to positive relationships between the two countries and other intangible benefits. Another benefit to U.S. businesses is that it gives them more market capacity where they obtain raw materials, finished products, or both, which provides for potential costs savings through the use of these additional choices for eventual sale to U.S. and other consumers. U.S. consumers benefit because countries determined to be equivalent are providing meat, poultry, and egg products that are as safe as domestic products because the products meet U.S. appropriate levels of protection. These additional products may also be less expensive than products produced with U.S.-sourced ingredients.

STRENGTHENING CAPACITY OF DEVELOPING COUNTRIES

Most agencies in our study provide technical assistance to developing countries. Agency officials said they work with countries to strengthen their regulatory systems, among other reasons, to improve safety of products imported into the United States.

Food and Drug Administration (FDA): Strengthening Global Regulatory Systems and Capacity

Agency: FDA

Description: FDA undertakes activities to improve the capacity of governments to manage, assess, and regulate products within increasingly complex supply chains. According to FDA officials, FDA works to strengthen the global regulatory system and is a source of expertise that engages in global dialogue and initiatives with regulatory counterparts, development agencies, and global health partners. FDA is developing an operating model that relies on building a global safety net using four principles: global coalitions, global data systems, enhanced risk analysis capacities, and leveraging the efforts of public and private third parties. FDA's Global Engagement Report outlines how FDA supports and collaborates with regulatory systems around the globe. While neither mandated nor funded as an international development or training organization, FDA works with bilateral and multilateral partners, domestically and internationally, to strengthen regulatory systems capacities and competencies in various parts of the world in an effort to ensure products that will be imported into the United States will be made safer and supply lines more secure. Examples of some of FDA's efforts include development of information-sharing platforms and the provision of evidence tools and expertise that contribute to strengthening regulatory systems.

- In response to Section 305 of the FDA Food Safety Modernization Act (FSMA), the FDA developed an international food-safety capacity- building plan. The plan establishes a strategic framework for the FDA and presents an approach based on prioritizing risks to U.S. consumers. It focuses on addressing weaknesses in a food safety system in partnership with foreign governments, industry counterparts, and other stakeholders.
- FDA supported the World Health Organization (WHO) in developing a global monitoring and surveillance system for substandard, falsified, and counterfeit medical products. The system was piloted in 10 countries over 3 months in 2012. This system will be scaled up globally in the coming year.
- FDA is actively involved in efforts to strengthen regulatory capacity through its joint efforts with the World Bank, the WHO, the Gates Foundation, Asia-Pacific Economic Cooperation (APEC), the African Union, and others in the private and public sectors. By bringing its regulatory and scientific expertise to these efforts, FDA can better leverage the expertise of its partners to engage more efficiently and broadly in enhancing regulatory capacity globally. Examples of such initiatives include the World Bank/APEC initiative on food-safety capacity building and the World Bank/Gates Foundation/WHO/ African Union efforts to enhance and rationalize regional regulatory capacity in various African economic communities, starting with the East African community.

Federal Trade Commission (FTC) Technical Assistance

Agency: FTC

Description: According to FTC officials, the FTC, in coordination with, among others, USAID, U.S. Trade and Development Agency, and the

Department of Commerce, establishes relationships with developing countries and provides technical assistance. FTC helps countries develop and enhance their regulatory frameworks by encouraging convergence with international standards. FTC's technical assistance program helps explain how competition, truthful advertising and marketing, and sensible privacy frameworks advance economic efficiency, consumer welfare, and consumer choice. To this end, FTC assists developing countries in their transition to market-based economies and their development of competition and consumer protection agencies and sharing approaches to enforcement that are consistent with this goal. As part of its efforts, the agency routinely provides input to its foreign counterparts about the drafting and adopting of domestic legislative frameworks regarding competition, consumer protection, and privacy. FTC also works to build the capacity of its foreign counterparts to implement these frameworks and promote their proper enforcement.

Animal and Plant Health Inspection Service (APHIS) Capacity Building

Agency: APHIS

Description: APHIS participates in international regulatory capacity building to help other regulatory entities meet U.S. standards and protect health. Officials said APHIS actively builds international partners and meets with foreign regulatory officials bilaterally and multilaterally. For example, APHIS runs six to seven courses a year where it invites foreign officials to the United States for training on U.S. processes. APHIS officials said that APHIS annually trains 100 to 150 individuals from other countries. The officials said these trainings provide education and resources to foreign counterparts and build a network of individuals to support U.S. efforts worldwide and help other countries comply with U.S. regulations. APHIS also participates in multilateral capacity building on SPS. Officials said, under the SPS agreement, there is a responsibility to work with developing countries and APHIS has officials located overseas who informally work with partners on a daily basis. APHIS also has formal training programs overseas and in the United States.

Work Sharing

Agencies work with foreign counterparts on projects to share resources to implement regulations and avoid duplicating efforts.

FDA Coordination on Inspections

Agency: FDA

Description: FDA partners with foreign counterparts to coordinate on inspection activities. Foreign counterparts include:

- European Medicines Agency (EMA): Significant opportunities exist for FDA and EMA to leverage their inspection resources, and they are exploring this potential through a series of activities. They observed each other's inspections and jointly inspected manufacturing sites in the United States and the European Union (EU). Through this work, FDA and EMA are building a foundation for understanding, trust, and data-driven decisions in the area of inspections.
- EMA and Australia's Therapeutic Goods Administration: In 2009, FDA joined the EMA and Australia's Therapeutic Goods Administration to conduct a pilot program—the Active Pharmaceutical Ingredient Inspection Pilot—to demonstrate the potential for leveraging their inspection resources. Before the pilot, these agencies had been conducting separate inspections at the same overseas manufacturing sites—often within just months of one another—to assure that the safety and quality of the drugs were not jeopardized by poor manufacturing practices. Under the pilot, the three agencies planned and conducted joint inspections at participating foreign facilities and shared information from inspections they had conducted over the past 2 to 3 years. These exchanges have allowed FDA to redeploy inspection resources and alerted FDA to sites requiring heightened scrutiny. Since then, FDA has engaged in similar projects with additional counterparts.
- Health Canada: FDA also works with Canada on Third-Party Inspection/Audits. To enable closer regulatory cooperation, FDA and Health Canada (HC) initiated the Pilot Multi-purpose Audit Program in 2006. The pilot explored the potential benefits to medical device manufacturers and the agencies of using a single third party for inspections audits to simultaneously meet FDA and HC regulatory requirements for systems quality. It was anticipated that a multipurpose audit could reduce the overall time spent on site by an official agency audit/inspection team, thus reducing the regulatory burden for industry. FDA and HC conducted 11 joint audit/

inspections under the pilot; 10 of these were assessed for program benefits. The results showed that the joint approach reduced the time-in-facility spent at participating manufacturers by about one-third, on average, compared with the estimated time required for separate FDA and HC audits/inspections. In addition, FDA and HC gained a better understanding of their auditing/inspection approaches, providing a foundation for leveraging inspection resources in the future.

- New Zealand's Ministry for Primary Industries: In December 2012, FDA signed an international arrangement with New Zealand's Ministry for Primary Industries recognizing each other's food safety systems as providing comparable degrees of food safety assurance. This arrangement was reached after a significant amount of time was spent by both parties working on regulatory systems recognition assessments. Systems recognition involves reviewing a foreign country's food safety regulatory system to determine if it provides a similar set of protections to that of FDA and that the food safety authority provides similar oversight and monitoring activities for food produced under its jurisdiction. Outcomes of these reviews may be used by FDA to make risk-based decisions regarding foreign inspections, admitting product into the U.S., and follow-up actions when food safety incidents occur.

Outcomes: Coordinated inspections allow FDA to leverage resources with their foreign counterparts to fulfill their regulatory responsibilities.

Joint Animal Health Site Visits to Third Countries

Agency: USDA's Animal and Plant Health Inspection Service (APHIS)

Description: As part of the United States-Canada Beyond the Border Initiative, APHIS and Canada conducted a joint site visit in Colombia for a foot and mouth disease evaluation and produced a joint report as part of the evaluation of Colombia's request to export fresh beef in October 2011. The United States and Canada are developing procedures for conducting future joint site visits and the exchange of information related to animal health evaluations. APHIS and Canada will also be identifying other opportunities to share evaluation results.

Outcomes: According to APHIS officials, outcomes could involve the United States and Canada developing risk evaluations that are based in part on a joint site visit.

Voluntary Programs

Agencies cooperate with foreign counterparts on voluntary programs that are not part of agencies' regulations.

Efficient Electrical End- use Equipment Implementing Agreement, Solid State Lighting Annex

Agency: Department of Energy (DOE)

Description: DOE's international coordination on solid state lighting is done in large part through the International Energy Agency (IEA) Efficient Electrical End-Use Equipment (4E) Implementing Agreement, which was launched in 2008 and undertakes a range of analytical and information gathering and dissemination activities related to government regulation and labeling of appliances and equipment. The IEA was established under the Agreement on International Energy Program. Thirteen countries from the Asia-Pacific, Europe, North America, and Africa have joined together under the forum of 4E to share information and transfer experience to support good policy development in the field of energy efficient appliances and equipment. 4E also initiates projects designed to meet the policy needs of participants, enabling better informed policy making.

Officials said they worked with the 4E Annex on Solid State Lighting for several years on performance characteristics and testing procedures during which time they developed a network of laboratories that would perform independent testing that could be voluntarily adopted by foreign governments. Solid state (or LED) lighting is a new technology that has cost and performance characteristics that are developing rapidly. The goal of the annex is to develop simple tools to help government and consumers worldwide identify which solid state lighting products have the necessary efficiencies and quality levels to reduce the amount of energy currently consumed by artificial lighting. DOE is working with other countries to identify efficiency and performance criteria and metrics, test methods, and qualified testing laboratories that might be used in product labeling or standards activities related to these products.

Outcomes: According to DOE officials, this coordination is important because the adoption of performance standards and test procedures will help determine the products that can be marketed and sold around the world. They said without a common agreement on key characteristics for this new technology, it would be difficult for products to enter the world market. Standard labeling helps customers understand the product they are buying and how its efficiency compares with other products. The results of cooperation on solid state lighting will not necessarily be reflected in DOE's regulations. DOE does not regulate this product at this time, although it has proposed a test procedure that might be used to support the Energy Star program or other initiatives.

End Notes

[1] Exec. Order No. 13534, National Export Initiative, 75 Fed. Reg. 12,433 (Mar. 16, 2010).

[2] Commerce officials pointed out that the term standard can have different meanings. For example, the term standard may be used to define a technical requirement or a technical standard, or refer to a regulatory requirement in the context of a model regulation, or refer to a commonly used general requirement. For simplicity, we use the term international standard throughout the remainder of this report.

[3] See GAO, *Consumer Product Safety Commission: Agency Faces Challenges in Responding to New Product Risks*, GAO-13-150 (Washington, D.C.: Dec. 20, 2012); *Food Safety: FDA Can Better Oversee Food Imports by Assessing and Leveraging Other Countries' Oversight Resources*, GAO-12-933 (Washington, D.C.: Sept. 28, 2012); and *Food Safety: Agencies Need to Address Gaps in Enforcement and Collaboration to Enhance Safety of Imported Food*, GAO-09-873 (Washington, D.C.: Sept. 15, 2009).

[4] GAO-09-873. In this report, we made 12 recommendations to improve the coordination, collaboration, information sharing, and screening systems supporting U.S. food safety programs, 9 of which have been implemented.

[5] The World Trade Organization (WTO) Agreement on Technical Barriers to Trade obligates WTO members to ensure that technical regulations are not prepared, adopted, or applied with a view to or with the effect of creating unnecessary obstacles to international trade. See Agreement on Technical Barriers to Trade, Apr. 15, 1994, Marrakesh Agreement Establishing the World Trade Organization, Annex 1A, Legal Instrument - Results of the Uruguay Round, 1868 U.N.T.S. 120 (1994) [hereinafter referred to as the TBT Agreement].

[6] The Unified Agenda provides uniform reporting of data on regulatory and deregulatory activities under development throughout the U.S. federal government. All entries in the online Unified Agenda contain uniform data elements, including "international impacts" (whether the regulation is expected to have international trade and investment effects, or otherwise may be of interest to the nation's international trading partners).

[7] USDA, which is a regulatory agency, also has a coordinating role as the national enquiry point for the World Trade Organization's Agreement on the Application of Sanitary and Phytosanitary Measures.

[8] GAO, *Managing for Results: Key Considerations for Implementing Interagency Collaborative Mechanisms*, GAO-12-1022 (Washington, D.C.: Sept. 27, 2012). To identify the key features, we conducted a literature review of academic work, interviewed a number of experts in governmental collaboration, and analyzed a sample of our prior work.

[9] Pub. L. No. 79-404, 60 Stat. 237 (1946), codified in 1966 in scattered sections of title 5, United States Code. Some agencies, such as CPSC, have statutory rulemaking requirements that add processes and steps beyond those required by the Administrative Procedure Act. See, *e.g., 13 U.S.C. § 2058.*

[10] The APA describes two types of rulemaking, formal and informal. Formal rulemaking includes a trial type "on-the-record" proceeding. Most federal agencies use the informal rulemaking procedures outlined in 5 U.S.C. § 553.

[11] A retrospective review of an existing rule may prompt this consideration.

[12] Exec. Order No. 12866, Regulatory Planning and Review, 58 Fed. Reg. 51,735 (Oct. 4, 1993).

[13] Executive Order 12866 defines significant regulatory actions to include those that are likely to result in a rule that may have an annual effect on the economy of $100 million or more or adversely affect in a material way the economy, or create a serious inconsistency or otherwise interfere with an action taken, or planned by another agency.

[14] This working group is chaired by the OIRA Administrator, and it consists of representatives of leadership in each agency that the OIRA Administrator has determined has significant domestic regulatory responsibility. Per Executive Order 13609, the RWG includes a representative from USTR and, as appropriate, representatives from other agencies and offices.

[15] Exec. Order No. 13563, Improving Regulation and Regulatory Review, 76 Fed. Reg. 3821 (Jan. 21, 2011).

[16] 19 U.S.C. § 3511.

[17] Fuller explanations of these agreements may be found at: http://www.wto.org/english/thewto_e/whatis_e/tif_e/agrm4_e.htm

[18] Specifically, TBT Agreement art. 2.2, 2.4, and 2.9.

[19] See Agreement on the Application of Sanitary and Phytosanitary Measures, Apr. 15, 1994, Marrakesh Agreement Establishing the World Trade Organization, Annex 1A, Legal Instrument - Results of the Uruguay Round, 1867 U.N.T.S. 493, 33 I.L.M. 1125 (1994) [hereinafter referred to as the SPS Agreement]. Specifically, SPS Agreement art. 2, 3, 5, 7, and Annexes A and B.

[20] The World Organization for Animal Health (formerly the Office International des Epizooties) is recognized by the SPS Agreement. Founded in 1924, the OIE has six main missions: (1) to ensure transparency in the global animal disease situation, (2) to collect, analyze and disseminate veterinary scientific information, (3) to provide expertise and encourage international solidarity in the control of animal diseases, (4) within its mandate under the WTO SPS Agreement, to safeguard world trade by publishing health standards for international trade in animals and animal products, (5) to improve the legal framework and resources of national veterinary services, and (6) to provide a better guarantee of food of animal origin and to promote animal welfare through a science-based approach.

[21] The International Organization for Standardization (ISO) is an independent, non- governmental organization made up of members from the national standards bodies of 163 countries and 3,368 technical bodies. International standards give specifications for products, services and good practice, in areas such as food safety, computers, agriculture, and health care.

[22] OECD, *International Regulatory Co-operation: Case Studies, Vol. 1: Chemicals, Consumer Products, Tax and Competition* (OECD Publishing: 2013), accessed 5/14/2013 http://dx.doi.org/10.1787/9789264200487-en.

[23] For more information on EPA's international efforts related to pesticides and food safety, see EPA, *The Value of Countries Working Together to Regulate Pesticides and Food Safety: Achieving Public Health and Environmental Protection through International Collaboration*, EPA 735-K0-9001 (Washington, D.C.: April 2009).

[24] Our prior work also found that coordination among domestic and foreign financial regulators improved the quality of rulemakings. For example, these coordination efforts likely eliminated duplication and helped fill regulatory gaps to limit risks migrating to unregulated markets. See GAO, *Financial Regulatory Reform: Regulators Have Faced Challenges Finalizing Key Reforms and Unaddressed Areas Pose Potential Risks*, GAO-13-195 (Washington, D.C.: Jan. 23, 2013).

[25] The General Services Administration's Regulatory Information Service Center and OMB's OIRA established Reginfo.gov to assist users who want to find federal regulatory information such as regulatory agendas and regulatory plans including brief synopses and timetables for action on rules that federal departments and agencies are considering. See http://www.reginfo.gov/public/.

[26] The federal government launched Regulations.gov in 2003 to enable citizens to search, view, and comment on regulations issued. See http://www.regulations.gov/#!home.

[27] 22 C.F.R. § 181.4(a).

[28] For example, USTR is required to coordinate international trade policy issues that arise as a result of implementation of the WTO TBT agreement. USTR is also required to inform and consult any federal agencies having expertise in the matters under discussion or negotiation in coordinating U.S. discussions and negotiations with foreign countries for the purpose of establishing mutual arrangements with respect to standards-related activities. USTR also must consult with the cited agency and members of the interagency trade organization if a foreign government makes a representation to the USTR alleging that a U.S. standards-related activity violates U.S. TBT obligations. Commerce and USDA must coordinate with USTR with respect to TBT international standards-related activities that may substantially affect the commerce of the United States. Furthermore, with regard to TBT obligations, the Secretaries of Commerce and USDA have a role in assuring adequate representation of U.S. interests in international standards organizations, and encouraging cooperation among federal agencies so as to facilitate development of a unified U.S. position.

[29] As of July 30, 2013 the guidance has not been issued.

[30] This is one of several key features outlined in GAO-12-1022.

[31] For example, Executive Order 13563 states that regulations shall be adopted through a process that involves public participation and shall be based, to the extent feasible and consistent with law, on the open exchange of information and perspectives. The executive order also states that before issuing a notice of proposed rulemaking, each agency, where feasible and appropriate, shall seek the views of those who are likely to be affected, including those who are likely to benefit from and those who are potentially subject to such rulemaking.

[32] Not all international regulatory cooperation activities result in regulations and not all regulations are significant.

[33] According to OMB officials, Executive Order 13579 recognizes that while not a requirement, independent agencies should follow these principles as well.

[34] The Volpe Center is part of DOT's Research and Innovative Technology Administration. Its mission is to improve the nation's transportation system by anticipating emerging transportation issues and to serve as a center of excellence for informed decision making.

[35] Legitimate objectives include: national security requirements; the prevention of deceptive practices; and protection of human health or safety, animal or plant life or health, or the environment. TBT Agreement, Art. 2.2 and 2.5.

[36] ASTM International was formerly known as the American Society for Testing and Materials.

[37] TBT Agreement art. 2.2, 2.4, and 2.6.

[38] Pub. L. No. 104-113, § 12(d).

[39] We have previously reported on CPSC's efforts related to voluntary standards, including international standards. See: GAO, *Consumer Product Safety Commission: A More Active Role in Voluntary Standards Development Should Be Considered*, GAO-12-582. (Washington, D.C.: May 21, 2012).

[40] These features include (1) outcomes and accountability; (2) bridging organizational cultures; (3) leadership; (4) clarity of roles and responsibilities; (5) participants; (6) resources; and (7) written guidance and agreements. In our collaboration work, we define collaboration as any joint activity that is intended to produce more public value than could be produced when organizations act alone. We use the term collaboration broadly to include interagency activities that others have variously defined as cooperation, coordination, integration, or networking. See GAO-12-1022 and GAO, *Results-Oriented Government: Practices That Can Help Enhance and Sustain Collaboration among Federal Agencies,* GAO-06-15 *(Washington, D.C.: Oct. 21, 2005).*

[41] GAO-12-1022.

[42] 19 U.S.C. § 2545.

[43] GAO-12-1022.

[44] GAO-12-1022.

[45] GAO-13-150.

[46] The Congressional Review Act defines a major rule as one that has resulted in or is likely to result in (1) an annual effect on the economy of $100 million or more; (2) a major increase in costs or prices for consumers, individual industries, federal, state, or local government agencies, or geographic regions; or (3) significant adverse effects on competition, employment, investment, productivity, or innovation, or on the ability of U.S.- based enterprises to compete with foreign-based enterprises in domestic and export markets. 5 U.S.C. § 804(2).

[47] Also including subagencies National Highway Traffic Safety Administration (NHTSA) and the Pipeline and Hazardous Materials Safety Administration (PHMSA).

[48] Also including subagencies Office of Air and Radiation (OAR) and the Office of Chemical Safety and Pollution Prevention (OCSPP).

[49] Also including subagencies Animal and Plant Health Inspection Service (APHIS), Agricultural Marketing Service (AMS), Food Safety and Inspection Service (FSIS), and Foreign Agricultural Service (FAS).

[50] USDA, which is a regulatory agency, also has a coordinating role as the national enquiry point for the World Trade Organization's Agreement on the Application of Sanitary and Phytosanitary Measures.

[51] GAO, *Managing for Results: Key Considerations for Implementing Interagency Collaborative Mechanisms*, GAO-12-1022 (Washington, D.C.: Sept. 27, 2012).

In: International Regulatory Cooperation
Editor: Lenore Lynch
ISBN: 978-1-63117-276-2

Chapter 2

TRANSATLANTIC REGULATORY COOPERATION: BACKGROUND AND ANALYSIS*

Raymond J. Ahearn

SUMMARY

Commercial ties between the United States and the 27-member European Union are substantial, growing, and mutually beneficial. However, differences in regulatory approaches limit an even more integrated marketplace from developing. To deal with this situation, a variety of government-to-government efforts have been created to dismantle existing regulatory barriers and to prevent new ones from emerging. These efforts fall under the rubric of transatlantic regulatory cooperation (TRC) and are at the heart of today's U.S.-EU economic relationship.

This report is intended to serve as an introduction and primer on a complicated, broad, and often highly technical set of issues. Since the mid-1990s, both U.S. and European multinational companies have viewed divergent ways of regulating markets for both goods and services as the most

---

* This is an edited, reformatted and augmented version of a Congressional Research Service Publication, CRS Report for Congress RL34717, dated December 22, 2011.

serious barriers to transatlantic commerce. The primary reason why these companies seek to achieve greater harmonization in standards and regulatory procedures is to reduce costs imposed by having to comply with two different sets of regulations and standards.

TRC must deal with a number of key differences between the United States and EU concerning approaches to regulation. These differences involve political support for regulation and public attitudes towards risk and transparency. Until they converge or are re-aligned, a transatlantic gap in regulatory policies is likely to persist.

Regulatory cooperation is an umbrella concept that incorporates a broad range of activities. At one end of the spectrum are information exchanges and dialogues among regulators that are designed to build trust and confidence. At the other end of the spectrum are activities designed to harmonize regulatory approaches through acceptance of common principles and standards. In between are activities that involve varying degrees of intrusion into the autonomy of regulators.

TRC initiatives have made progress in reducing costs to businesses and consumers in some sectors, but not in others. One of the key obstacles to more extensive cooperation frequently cited is the domestic orientation of regulatory agencies involved in the process. To promote more effective TRC, two policy options are commonly advanced: (1) attracting high-level political support and (2) increasing dramatically the involvement of legislators (Congress and the European Parliament). The Transatlantic Economic Council (TEC), which was created in April 2007, was designed, in part, to generate the kind of high-level political support that previous initiatives may have lacked.

At the last TEC meeting, held in November 2011, the two sides agreed to avoid creating new and unintended barriers to trade and investment, especially in emerging technologies, such as nanotechnology, biobased food, and cloud computing. The leaders also encouraged regulators on both sides to implement common regulatory principles and best practices.

TRC has been mostly an executive branch driven process. Yet, through authorization and appropriations of the many different regulatory agencies involved in TRC, Congress could play a more central role if it decided to move in this direction. As domestic regulation takes place in an increasingly integrated transatlantic marketplace, Congress will be called upon to balance the often competing demands of trade expansion and barrier reduction against domestic health and safety concerns.

INTRODUCTION

The United States and the 27-Member European Union (EU) share a huge, dynamic, and mutually beneficial economic partnership.[1] Not only is the U.S.-EU commercial relationship, what many call the transatlantic economy, the largest in the world, it is also arguably the most important.[2] While the transatlantic market is today highly integrated due in large part to a massive amount of foreign direct investment by both U.S. and European companies in each other's markets, differences in regulatory approaches, standards, and philosophies militate against the development of an even tighter and more integrated marketplace. Regulatory differences are also behind some of the most politically sensitive bilateral trade disputes.

To deal with this situation, a variety of government-to-government efforts and transatlantic dialogues have been created to increase understanding between policymakers and regulators on both sides of the Atlantic, to minimize existing regulatory barriers, and to prevent the emergence of new regulatory barriers. These efforts, falling under the rubric of transatlantic regulatory cooperation (TRC), are seen as being important to today's U.S.-EU economic relationship. Proponents maintain that TRC undertakings can not only prevent disruptive and costly trade disputes from occurring, but also spur trade and investment flows by reducing costs for producers and consumers on both sides of the Atlantic.

Since the establishment of the New Transatlantic Agenda (NTA) in 1995, there have been a number of new TRC initiatives, all aimed at removing or reducing regulatory barriers to trade.[3] While each of these initiatives has made some progress toward reducing regulatory burdens, many U.S. and European companies heavily engaged in the transatlantic marketplace maintain that the results have not been materially significant.

At the 2007 U.S.-EU Summit, leaders of the EU and United States committed their governments to increasing the efficiency and transparency of transatlantic economic cooperation and to accelerating the reduction and elimination of barriers to international trade and investment with the ultimate objective of achieving a barrier free transatlantic market. They also agreed on a Framework for Advancing Transatlantic Economic Integration (the Framework) and created a new institutional structure, the Transatlantic Economic Council (TEC), to advance the process of regulatory cooperation and barrier reduction. Headed on both sides by ministerial-level appointees, the TEC is designed to oversee the efforts outlined in the Framework, with the goal of accelerating progress and guiding work between the Summits.[4]

Whether the TEC will herald a new era of more effective cooperation remains to be seen. Much could depend upon whether the TEC can exert enough political leverage to convince regulators to make reforms that will result in reduction of regulatory barriers between the EU and the United States, as well as increase the role that legislators on both sides of the Atlantic play in the process. Six TEC meetings have been held since it was established in 2007, the most recent in November 2011 in Washington, DC.

This report is intended to serve as an introduction and primer on a complicated, broad, and often highly technical set of issues. It is presented in seven parts: the first section describes the nature and scope of U.S.-EU regulatory barriers; the second section explains the rationale for regulatory cooperation; the third section highlights the differences in U.S.-EU regulatory approaches; the fourth section examines the various forms of regulatory cooperation; the fifth section evaluates the results of past initiatives at regulatory cooperation; the sixth section analyzes the creation and operation of the Transatlantic Economic Council; and the last section highlights the role of Congress in transatlantic regulatory cooperation.

U.S.-EU Regulatory Barriers

Since the mid-1990s, both U.S. and European multinational companies (MNCs) have viewed divergent ways of regulating markets for both goods and services as the most serious barriers to transatlantic commerce. Redundant standards, testing, and certification procedures are seen by these companies as far more costly and harmful than any trade barriers imposed at the border, such as tariffs or quotas. While the purpose of many regulations is to protect consumers and the environment, divergent domestic regulations and standards can affect the competitive position of firms, helping some and disadvantaging others by affecting the importation of products not produced or grown according to those requirements.[5]

To the extent that product standards differ, exporters may find their goods prohibited from certain markets or subject to expensive re-labeling, re-packaging, or re-testing. For example, European winemakers intending to sell in the U.S. market must label their bottles according to U.S. requirements, which are different than EU requirements. Similarly, U.S. exports to the EU of poultry washed with anti-microbial treatments have been blocked for years by different health and safety standards.

Different regulations add to the cost of doing business on both sides of the Atlantic and serve as non-tariff barriers to trade in many different economic activities and sectors. These include but certainly are not limited to differences in accounting and financial reporting requirements, antitrust or competition procedures, consumer protection (safety and health) standards, environmental regulations, and personal data transmission. Each of these divergences can materialize into politically charged disputes and threaten the functioning of the transatlantic market.

In no area has this been a greater problem than in chemicals. In this sector, the United States and EU have fundamentally different regulations on issues such as genetically modified organisms (GMOs), hormones, and the registration and restriction of chemical substances. In the case of GMOs, these differences have translated into longer authorization times and stricter standards for approval, release, and marketing of GMOs in the EU than in the United States Moreover, GMOs have been the subject of a long and bitter trade dispute brought before the World Trade Organization.[6]

Pharmaceuticals is another sector where regulatory differences have been described as not only significant, but also bewildering. Just in the area of drug approvals, primary regulatory elements governing testing protocols, submission of clinical data, and certification of good manufacturing practices vary considerably between the United States and EU. Moreover, within the EU, where public health policy is still a national prerogative, rules and protocols can vary greatly from member state to member state. Because each member state has its own rules and protocols, it can be quite expensive for pharmaceutical companies to achieve marketing authorization throughout the EU or even a subset of countries.[7]

Another example comes from the automotive sector, where American and European car makers sell similar products in the United States and Europe. But there are different standards and testing requirements for all kinds of parts, ranging from headlights, wiper blades, light beams, and seat belts to crash standards—which critics maintain are without measurable differences in safety benefits. There are even multiple crash test dummies of the same or similar size and purpose—a clear example of where regulatory requirements diverge.[8]

Despite the salience of regulatory barriers in transatlantic commerce, a comprehensive, sector-by- sector study or inventory of regulatory barriers has not been undertaken. Proponents argue that such a report could identify regulatory differences that impose substantial burdens on transatlantic commerce and possibilities for their reduction or convergence without compromising either U.S. or EU health and safety priorities. In 2003, the European Commission (EC) proposed that such a study be undertaken and jointly funded, but the U.S. government did not back the initiative. Both sides, however, note the major regulatory divergences that are considered trade barriers in their respective annual trade barrier reports. In the 2008 U.S. trade barriers report, for example, 12 pages are devoted specifically to EU regulatory barriers.[9]

Rationale for Transatlantic Regulatory Cooperation

Efforts to enhance TRC draw on both economic and political justifications and are strongly supported by business interests and governments on both sides of the Atlantic. At the same time, within the United States, some interests, mostly academics, see greater benefits derived from regulatory competition and independence, whereby each side is free to maintain its own approach to regulating consumer, health, and environmental issues. The case for non-cooperation or at least caution is also based on concerns that domestic health and safety standards may be compromised by a process that is driven substantially by business interests and stakeholders and could be affected by a "race to the bottom" regarding U.S. and EU standards.

Economic Rationale

The primary reason why many export industries seek to achieve greater harmonization in international standards is to reduce costs associated with complying with two different sets of regulations and standards. To the extent that transatlantic regulatory standards and procedures differ, the costs of engaging in transatlantic commerce increase.[10]

A good example comes from the auto industry. According to a trade association, a U.S.-based producer of light trucks looked into exporting a model to Europe and found that its design was incompatible with a European regulation on exterior edge projection (the United States has no comparable standard). The truck was never exported because it would have required a major and costly re-design. The same truck manufacturer then undertook to ensure that another model on the drawing boards would have maximum export potential built into its design. In order to sell this product in Europe, the manufacturer reportedly utilized 100 unique parts, incurred an additional $42 million in design and developmental costs, and committed an additional 130 people to the program. Yet, the performance of the vehicle, in terms of safety, was unchanged. European-based manufacturers face the same issues in reverse when contemplating selling a European-designed model in the United States. These separate regulations, in turn, may cost manufactures millions of extra dollars to comply with, but may result in no changes in the vehicle in terms of safety or fuel economy.[11]

A 2005 OECD study is often cited to illustrate how costly regulatory barriers are to producers and consumers on both sides of the Atlantic. This study estimates that regulatory divergences between the United States and Europe costs the United States a sum that is equivalent to 1%-3% of GDP annually.[12]

In addition to cost savings that might be derived from the harmonization of regulations so as to facilitate open markets, it is argued that regulatory cooperation between states will help ensure that regulatory standards will not serve as obstacles to freer trade or unfair trade advantages.[13]

Just as internal regulatory divergences can become a source of competitive advantage or trade tension, proponents of regulatory convergence assert that differences in emissions standards, labeling requirements, and attitudes towards public health risks between countries can become a market access barrier for foreign products or provide domestic producers with “unfair” competitive advantages.

Proponents of regulatory cooperation maintain that it could have the effect of preventing a welfare-reducing “race to the bottom” as jurisdictions seek to advance the competitiveness of their own industries through lax regulation or lower standards. This rationale for regulatory cooperation served to justify a large expansion of federal legislation and institutions in the United States in the areas of environmental regulation, consumer protection, health and safety, and labor protections. Similar fears of trade distortions and races to the bottom led to the implementation of sweeping harmonization programs and centralized legislation in the EU.[14]

Cast in the context of the global economy, some view TRC as a way for the United States and EU to promote global regulatory standards. In the absence of world standards, the United States and Europe are often competing for acceptance of their respective regulations in third markets. Proponents of

TRC indicate that the net effect of this competition is that India and China can play the United States off against Europe, developing their own technical standards and financial regulations, complicating world trade for everyone.[15]

Political Rationale

Supporters of TRC note that since the end of the Cold War, the United States and Europe have been searching for various ways to bolster the foundation of the relationship. Absent the common enemy embodied in the threat posed by the former Soviet Union, both sides have felt freer to pursue their own narrow economic and political interests. In the process, trade disputes have appeared to increase in frequency, focusing often on differences in regulation, rather than the traditional barriers of tariffs and subsidies.

To deal with the joint task of giving the relationship a new rationale as well as bolstering overall ties, numerous attempts have been made since the 1995 NTA to enhance transatlantic economic cooperation. In this context, efforts to advance regulatory cooperation have been part of attempts to reinvigorate and upgrade the bilateral relationship. Annual summits, attended by the U.S. President, the President of the European Commission, and the President of the European Council, have been the venue for bringing high-level political attention and focus on efforts to enhance transatlantic regulatory cooperation. Regulatory cooperation, now entailing an expanding group of stakeholders and networks, has become a significant component of the U.S.-EU economic relationship. Supporters argue that through such cooperation the partners may be able to find ways to amicably and expeditiously resolve commercial disputes, as well as establish joint approaches to a number of common regulatory challenges that have global importance.[16]

Because the United States and European Union collectively represent over 50% of global production, in areas where they can agree on a common regulatory policy or approach, they are well-positioned to promote it globally. Where they disagree, there is often deadlock, reflecting the equal size of their economies and markets.[17]

While there are other forums (such as the World Trade Organization and international treaties) to promote regulatory cooperation, they are seen as having shortcomings. The WTO, for example, promotes regulatory cooperation by giving some international standards legal effect, nudging WTO Members to actively participate in international standardization bodies. It also puts national provisions to the test in various committees and offers its members a platform to facilitate regulatory cooperation.[18] But the number of transatlantic regulatory differences that fall within the scope of WTO rules constitute a relatively small proportion of the regulatory policies and procedures that involve firms on both sides of the Atlantic. Moreover, the few regulatory-based trade disputes that the WTO has decided sometimes exacerbate rather than lessen tensions between the United States and EU.[19] For this reason, it is argued that the United States and EU need to develop bilateral mechanisms for coordinating their regulatory policies.[20]

Counter-Arguments

Although there is strong support for TRC among business and government leaders on both sides of the Atlantic, the concept and rationale have their critics. This opposition is based, in part, on an alternative view of the benefits of regulatory competition as opposed to a centrally adopted regulatory framework constructed through regulatory cooperation. These mostly academic critics see benefits in variations in regulatory approaches across jurisdictions (either intra-state or interstate) as a way of disciplining overarching governments and creating incentives for bureaucratic efficiency. They argue that regulatory competition leads to the adoption of standards of varying stringency that efficiently match the needs and desires of each jurisdiction. Because conditions, tastes, and incomes tend to vary across jurisdictions, this school of thought maintains that an optimal regulatory policy for one jurisdiction will not necessarily be optimal for another.

Some consumer groups caution against the influential role that business groups play in transatlantic regulatory cooperation. The concern is that safety and health concerns may be compromised if business groups play such a prominent role in negotiations over testing requirements and standards for their own products. Rather than reducing barriers per se, the Trans-Atlantic Consumers Dialogue maintains that the purpose of regulatory cooperation between the United States and EU should be to promote higher health and safety standards, thereby improving consumer welfare on both sides of the Atlantic.[21]

Opponents of TRC assert from this perspective that a great number of centralized regulatory programs should be dismantled and regulatory powers should be decentralized. They believe that regulatory cooperation also reaches its limits where there is lack of institutional architecture to enforce decisions.[22]

U.S.-EU DIFFERENCES IN REGULATORY APPROACHES

Transatlantic regulatory cooperation must deal with a number of key differences between the United States and EU concerning approaches to regulation. Key differences bear on political cycles affecting regulation, public preferences and tolerance for risk, attitudes towards transparency, and institutional capacities to undertake regulatory reforms. These key differences—whether they pertain to product safety, environmental protection, securities trading, or customs procedures—in how regulations are developed and applied, in turn, raise challenges about whether and how to merge, harmonize, or converge the varied approaches. Until the regulatory structures themselves become more convergent or aligned, the major divergences in regulatory policies are unlikely to disappear.

Political Cycles

Over the last 50 years, the political cycles of regulatory policy stringency and expansion in the EU and the United States have not moved together. In the process, many important European and American regulations have diverged.[23]

Beginning in the 1960s, many U.S. regulatory standards were likely more comprehensive and stringent than those adopted by the EU and most member states. The United States was typically first to identify new consumer and environmental risks and more likely to adopt relatively risk- averse or precautionary standards for dealing with those risks. For example, from the early 1960s through the mid-1980s, American standards for the approval of new pharmaceutical products were more stringent than in any EU member state, and American automobile emission standards were consistently more stringent than those adopted in Europe. The United States also restricted the use of lead in gasoline more rapidly than did Europe and also acted more aggressively to restrict the use of ozone-depleting chemicals.[24]

But over the last 15 years, a number of European standards have become more stringent and comprehensive than U.S. standards.[25] For example, European standards for the approval and labeling of genetically modified (GM) foods and seeds are far more stringent than those adopted by the United States. Recently approved legislation on chemicals (Registration, Evaluation, and Authorization of Chemicals or REACH) has made European standards for the approval of both existing and new chemicals much more demanding than in the United States. The EU has also moved more aggressively than the United States to impose restrictions on greenhouse gas emissions.

However, in the aftermath of rising concerns about the safety of imported products and the financial crisis caused by the proliferation of sub-prime mortgages, support for more aggressive regulatory actions is rising in the United States. If the pendulum in the United States swings back towards increased regulation, this may narrow some of the current transatlantic regulatory divergences.[26]

Values and Public Preferences

Some transatlantic regulatory differences reflect different public preferences and values. For example, many European consumers tend to prefer "naturally produced" foods, while many American consumers are more accepting of products produced by advanced forms of agricultural production. This difference helps to explain, in part, why Europe has imposed restrictions on the use of growth hormones for both beef and dairy cows, while the United States has not. It also explains, in part, the relative lack of political controversy in the United States surrounding the introduction of biotechnology compared to the more negative response to this technology in Europe.[27]

The United States and EU also operate two different systems of risk management. As in the case of GMOs, the U.S. system is relatively science-based and prefers to regulate once significant problems have been identified. This approach has strong support of farmers, industry, and government officials. On the European side, the public tends to favor a more cautious approach, preferring to regulate out of precaution before a problem has occurred. The food safety scandals of the 1990s increased the resolve of EU member governments to put in place ever more strict regulation for the pre-approval, traceability, and labeling of all GMOs, independent of their individual safety characteristics.[28]

Transparency and Rule-Making

The United States and EU provide for very different degrees of public participation in rule- making. In the United States, Congress passes laws, but generally grants broad authority to the administrative or regulatory agencies to implement those laws through regulations. On occasion, Congress also provides specific direction to these agencies.

Regulations proposed by U.S. administering agencies are subject to considerable public input due in large part to the requirements of the U.S. Administrative Procedures Act (APA), the Freedom of Information Act, and the Government in the Sunshine Act, which permit public scrutiny of regulatory activity. A myriad of laws, executive orders, and bulletins ensure that transparency remains part of the regulatory process. Federal agencies are required to publish in the Federal Register, not just the proposed rule, but the supporting justification for the rule and the entire analytic justification behind it.

EU directives (which serve the same function as U.S. regulations) tend to be developed by the European Commission without as much input from either the public, business, or elected officials. The European Parliament, however, has to approve or pass the directives (legislation) proposed by the Commission. While the EU has a number of "better regulation" procedures and guidelines, it has no effective equivalent to the APA.[29]

Recognizing that the United States and EU have become each other's most important stakeholder, both sides may have an interest in ensuring that the other will have the opportunity, method, and forum for participating constructively in each other's regulatory process.

Institutional Capacity to Undertake Reforms

There also major differences in institutional capacities to undertake regulatory reforms. The EU's institutional framework is well suited to making regulatory changes. In broad terms, the EU has developed as a regulatory state with the European Commission taking a leading role in coordinating European wide regulatory policies in pursuit of building a Single Market. The Commission has ample authority to coordinate cooperation on transatlantic regulatory issues. The regulatory culture within the EU internal market is considered "trade friendly" because EU and national regulators operate with dual missions to promote free trade within the internal market while ensuring public safety. But enforcement is usually left to member states, which often results in a different levels of enforcement and different treatment of European and U.S. companies.[30]

In general, U.S. regulatory agencies have the mandate and funding to focus on domestic regulatory issues and they enjoy a fair amount of independence on policy and implementation matters. However, the United States lacks a clear-cut institutional mechanism to coordinate cooperative efforts. And neither the Commerce Department nor the Office of U.S. Trade Representative (USTR), the lead agencies for U.S. undertakings in the realm of transatlantic regulatory cooperation, have authority to overhaul domestic regulatory policymaking. While Commerce and USTR may bring the heads of U.S. regulatory agencies to the negotiating table, the regulatory agencies are not usually funded nor mandated to engage in TRC activities.[31]

An added structural complication on the U.S. side is the role that states play in regulating activities, particularly professional services. Insurance, banking, private pension fund management, and professional services such as engineering and architecture are all subject to state regulation (and some sectors exclusively).[32]

FORMS OF TRANSATLANTIC REGULATORY COOPERATION

Regulatory cooperation is an elastic concept that subsumes a broad range of activities. At one end of the spectrum, these activities may include simple discussions and sharing of information between regulators—most often on prospective regulations. At the other end of the spectrum, these activities may involve attempts at harmonizing regulatory approaches through acceptance of common principles and standards. In between are activities that involve varying degrees of intrusion into the autonomy of regulators. One such category is agreements that recognize each other's standards or certification procedures. These agreements are known as MRAs or mutual recognition agreements. The line between each category can be arbitrary and vague, and there are other activities associated with regulatory cooperation that may not fall neatly into one of the above categories.[33]

To date, most efforts at transatlantic regulatory cooperation have been associated with information exchanges and dialogues. Considerable efforts have also been made at negotiating MRAs for a range of goods, as well as other attempts to recognize the adequacy of each others standards in specific areas such as data privacy and accounting. Little has been undertaken in regard to harmonization of standards. What follows is a short elaboration of activities that apply to each of these regulatory activities.

Information Exchanges and Dialogues

The most basic form of regulatory cooperation involves the establishment of a working group or dialogue for an exchange of information. The group, which may be comprised of technical experts or regulators from different jurisdictions, may meet on an ad hoc and informal basis or may be more structured. A primary objective of these consultations may be to better understand technical differences in standards or regulations and to consult with each other prior to new regulations becoming effective.

Making an effort to work with or consult with each other prior to new regulations becoming effective is viewed as one way to minimize unnecessary regulatory barriers. The exchange of people and information is also expected to build trust and confidence, with the hope of making for more informed and coordinated regulations and may eventually lead to agreement on what constitutes best regulatory practice.

While an exchange of views and a discussion of different issues will not necessarily bring about a meeting of the minds in the technical assessment of a certain field of regulation, it is a necessary first step if convergence is to take place. Where there is no attempt at dialogue, efforts to restrain unilateral legislative actions that could create new regulatory barriers are unlikely to be successful.[34]

In the transatlantic context, a number of U.S. regulatory agencies (e.g., the Securities and Exchange Commission, the Food and Drug Administration, the National Highway Traffic Administration, and the Occupational Safety and Health Administration) have engaged in these kinds of information exchanges and non-binding dialogues with their European counterparts over the past decade. These exchanges were encouraged by the *Guidelines on Regulatory Cooperation and Transparency* which the United States and EU negotiated as part of the 1998 Transatlantic Economic Partnership (TEP). The guidelines were intended to enhance cooperation between EU and U.S. regulators in the development of technical regulations and specifically referred to regular consultation, exchange of data and information, as well as informing one another at an early stage on planned new regulation.

Since 2004, the annual U.S.-EU summits have reinforced efforts at regulatory cooperation. A *Roadmap for Regulatory Cooperation* provides a framework of specific activities in 15 different sectors (e.g., pharmaceuticals, telecommunications equipment, food safety, and auto safety). Subsequent summits have prescribed cooperation for "lighthouse projects" in the fields of intellectual property rights, secure trade, financial markets, innovation, and technology, as well as the elimination of obstacles to investment. In addition, a *High Level Regulatory Cooperation Forum,* comprised of regulators from both sides, was established to find common ground on horizontal issues such as risk assessment, cost-benefit analysis, and impact analysis when promulgating regulations.

Mutual Recognition Agreements

A stronger form of cooperation involves MRAs. This cooperation entails an agreement by regulators to accept products or services from another jurisdiction under specified conditions, so that actors complying with the regulations of one jurisdiction will be considered to be in compliance with the rules in another jurisdiction. These kind of agreements can focus on the mutual recognition of conformity assessment certifications or the alignment of relevant standards.

Under full recognition of standards, companies, for example, could sell pharmaceuticals in the United States after meeting European standards without first obtaining FDA approval. An agreement on conformity assessment procedures is a smaller step, requiring domestic regulators to accept the competency of their foreign counterparts to conduct product testing, inspection, or certification. The basic premise behind this kind of MRA is that products could be tested once and considered to have been tested in both markets.[35]

In 1998, the United States and EU completed an MRA for testing and certification requirements covering multiple sectors, including telecommunications and information technology equipment, pharmaceuticals, electronics, electromagnetic compatibility, sports boats, and medical devices. The MRA did not provide for mutual recognition of product standards, but it identified certification bodies in the exporting country that could assess the conformity of a range of traded goods with standards of the destination country. The MRAs, thus, introduced competition between assessors or certification bodies.

Competition among certification entities was familiar in Europe, where private firms had long provided certification, but was new in the United States, where government agencies had dominated the process. As a result, while some U.S. officials believed that the MRAs would lead to cheaper and more rapid certification, others were concerned about its implications for product safety.[36]

The MRAs did not result in any kind of binding legal agreement between the United States and the EU. Rather they were accomplished through an exchange of letters between the heads of the relevant regulatory agencies. To be implemented successfully, MRAs require that regulators on both sides of the Atlantic have confidence that the other side will not try to attract more business by being deliberately lax. Similarly, regulators need to recognize that each other's safety standards and inspection requirements are basically equivalent.[37]

Harmonization/Agreement on Regulatory Standards

The strongest form of regulatory cooperation involves harmonization or agreement on the same standards or rules applied across jurisdictions. This could extend not only to regulatory targets (e.g., the permissible level of a particular pollutant in each jurisdiction or reserve requirements among banks), but also to the manner by which regulators ensure compliance with their regulations.

In the transatlantic context, few precedents exist for acceptance or adoption of similar or identical standards. While there have been numerous political declarations calling for regulatory convergence and harmonization, few changes have been enacted in each side's existing laws that would move their regulatory regimes in this direction. The transatlantic market, of course, is not a single market with common institutions pushing for further economic integration. But various stakeholders, frustrated by the slow progress in transatlantic regulatory cooperation, have made proposals that could push the two sides in the direction of adopting a new institutional architecture, such as a binding regulatory cooperation agreement.[38]

Those who see a binding treaty or regulatory cooperation agreement as necessary institutional architecture to achieve a transatlantic single market point to EU integration as a model. In moving towards the completion of a Single European Market, the Commission issued a white paper that listed the pieces of legislation requiring harmonization, and simultaneously identified the institutional mechanisms to achieve specified ends.[39]

U.S. public support for such an approach could depend on whether the goal of such a treaty or legal agreement was the development of identical legislation or comparable legislation. If the goal was identical legislation, much resistance to this kind of deeper integration could be expected from a number of quarters. This is particularly true from stakeholders who view movement in this direction as leading to a loss of regulatory autonomy for U.S. authorities. If the goal was the development of similar or comparable legislation that facilitates mutual recognition, much less resistance perhaps could be expected.[40]

RESULTS OF PAST INITIATIVES AT REGULATORY COOPERATION

The United States and EU have pursued a variety of policy initiatives and new mechanisms over the past 15 years to reduce or eliminate regulatory barriers. The results have been mixed. A number of these initiatives have been successful in some regulatory areas, while transatlantic regulatory cooperation has not made material differences for businesses or consumers in some other sectors. Assuming it is concluded that stronger regulatory cooperation is desirable, an assessment of past efforts could be useful.

Highlights of Past Initiatives

Beginning in 1990 with the Transatlantic Declaration, regular U.S.-EU summits were initiated to reinvigorate and upgrade the bilateral relationship. Attended by the U.S. President, the President of the European Commission, and the President of the European Council, the summits were intended to bring high-level focus to cooperative activities. Successive summits have led to a number of agreements relating to transatlantic regulatory cooperation:

- At the 1995 summit in Madrid, the United States and EU formally adopted the New Transatlantic Agenda (NTA) in an effort to provide a new foundation for the partnership. The NTA was accompanied by a detailed action plan. In addition, the NTA set up a comprehensive and regular government-to-government dialogue, as well as four dialogues between stakeholders on both sides of the Atlantic. These included the Transatlantic Business Dialogue (TABD), the Transatlantic Labor Dialogue (TALD), the Transatlantic Environmental Dialogue (TAED) and the Transatlantic Consumer Dialogue (TACD).

- Pursuant to the NTA, the two sides focused particular attention on problems posed by divergent standards and certification systems. In addition to promoting the convergence in regulatory systems, efforts were undertaken to negotiate MRAs covering several sectors. In 1998, MRAs affecting sectors such as electrical equipment, pharmaceutical products, telecommunications, and information technology equipment were reached.
- At the 1998 summit in London, the Transatlantic Economic Partnership (TEP) was created to improve bilateral economic and trade relations and to help create a more open world trading system. The TEP established deadlines for particular actions within the areas of regulatory cooperation, mutual recognition, and consumer product safety.
- At the Bonn Summit in June 1999, a Joint Statement on *Early Warning and Problem Prevention Mechanisms* was adopted. The warning system was designed to identify regulations, preferably still in draft form, that might contribute to non- tariff barriers to trade.
- At the 2000 U.S.-EU Summit in Lisbon, the Consultative Forum on Biotechnology was established to improve communication and understanding on the various concerns involved in biotechnology.
- At the May 2002 summit in Washington, the two sides reached agreements on *Guidelines for Regulatory Cooperation and Transparency*. These sought to take the idea of an early warning system a step further by encouraging U.S. and EU regulatory agencies to consult on a voluntary basis, sharing work plans that identify areas of anticipated regulatory action for the coming year and offering opportunities for reaction before regulations are finalized.[41]
- Moving towards a more systematic cooperative approach, a *Roadmap for EU-U.S. Regulatory Cooperation and Transparency* was developed in June 2004. It listed 10 specific projects for regulatory discussion and also expanded the approach to horizontal initiatives.
- The 2005 EU-U.S. Summit produced a second *Roadmap for EU-U.S. Regulatory Cooperation and Transparency* and expanded the list to 15 sector-specific projects. It also established two new dialogues. One was between the European Commission and Office of Management and Budget on transparency and methodologies for impact and risk assessment, in order to improve understanding of each other's regulatory systems. A second, a *High-Level Regulatory Cooperation Forum*, was tasked to develop a joint regulatory work plan based on

mutual best practices. Its members include senior U.S. and European Commission officials, academics, business executives, and other officials.

Accomplishments

Among the accomplishments are the following:

1. Most observers would agree that new mechanisms for dialogue and information exchange have improved mutual understanding and day-to-day working relationships among economic regulators in a wide range of sectors; Arguably, cooperation is now far deeper, broader, more decentralized and routine than it had been before in areas such as pharmaceuticals, medical devices, financial services, and marine equipment.
2. The NTA process and related efforts at regulatory cooperation fostered closer relationships among many stakeholders, including business people representing the major corporations investing in both Europe and the United States. In particular, the TABD, representing a transatlantic coalition of big businesses on both sides of the Atlantic, developed into an "effective framework for enhanced cooperation between the transatlantic business community and the governments of the European Union and the United States."[42]
3. The NTA and subsequent summits enhanced on-going efforts to increase the compatibility of U.S. and EU approaches to competition policy. According to one observer, much convergence in substantive standards has been achieved voluntarily through the exchange of ideas and institutional learning processes.[43]
4. MRAs (discussed previously) covering over $50 billion in trade were implemented in three sectors, leading to significant cost savings for U.S. businesses; several of the agreements provided for U.S. and EU testing facilities to recognize each other's standards over time, thus allowing firms to have products tested only once on either side of the Atlantic. The Commerce Department estimated that the agreement would save U.S. industries more than $1 billion in testing and certification costs.[44]
5. The 2002 *Guidelines for Regulatory Cooperation* promoted a number of procedural steps that most likely have facilitated a more effective

dialogue. These steps included arrangements to permit sharing of non-public information between regulators. The *Roadmap for Regulatory Cooperation* now provides a framework for consultations and dialogue in 15 different sectors (e.g., pharmaceuticals, telecommunications equipment, food safety, and auto safety) with a focus on prospective regulations and reducing regulatory barriers.

6. The U.S.-EU Safe Harbor Agreement was implemented in 2002. This agreement provided an innovative mechanism whereby U.S. firms could be certified as meeting the EU's more demanding data privacy requirements for exporting personal data.
7. In February 2004, the United States and EU signed an MRA on marine safety equipment covering $150 million to $200 million annually in two-way trade.[45]
8. The *U.S.-EU High Level Regulatory Cooperation Forum,* established in 2005, has focused on methodologies for generating good regulatory practices. To the extent both sides are able to develop a methodological framework that ensures the comparability of regulatory reviews, with an emphasis on risk assessments, cost/benefit analysis, and trade and investment impacts, unilateral legislative initiatives, and the creation of new regulatory barriers can be curtailed.
9. By 2006 the Financial Markets Regulatory Dialogue had reported some progress on recognizing each others' financial standards in specific areas.[46] In particular, progress has been made on gaining the mutual acceptance by 2009 of the equilevance of accounting standards—that is, the U.S. Generally Accepted Accounting Principles (GAAP) and International Financial Reporting Standards (IFRS). This will make it easier for European companies to raise capital in the United States and for U.S. companies to raise capital in Europe.[47]

Disappointments

Specific disappointments include the following.

1. Enthusiasm for mutual recognition as a regulatory strategy faded when three of the six agreements failed to become operational by established deadlines.[48] In the view of some analysts, these MRAs

were never implemented due to the U.S. reluctance to recognize the equivalency of European certifiers. In the pharmaceutical and medical device sectors, for example, the FDA had continuing doubts about the capability of some EU member states to oversee high pharmaceutical standards in laboratories. In the electrical equipment sector, OSHA refused to cede its right to designate which laboratories in Europe could evaluate and certify new electrical products for sale in the United States.[49] A related obstacle on the European side was the EU inclination to regulate at the European level, only to leave enforcement to Member States, which often results in different levels of enforcement and different treatment of European and U.S. companies.[50]

2. Irrespective of annual summits, the TEP, by some accounts, went into hibernation from 1998 to 2004. Despite the many recommendations and political declarations issued during this time period, there were few material accomplishments.[51]
3. Pieces of legislation adopted unilaterally by both sides in 2002 served to put a break on regulatory cooperation by violating the *2002 Guidelines on Regulatory Cooperation* and the *"Early Warning System."* On the one side, the EU imposed its views on how to regulate chemicals by adopting legislation known as REACH, which affected the testing and approval of chemicals, without much input from U.S. stakeholders. On the other side, the United States adopted legislation (Sarbanes-Oxley), which reformed public accounting standards, without taking into account EU views. Both pieces of legislation created considerable difficulties for transatlantic businesses, from companies attempting to raise capital to firms that manufacture everyday goods.
4. Despite extensive efforts at cooperation for nearly two decades, the transatlantic regulatory divide remains large in the area of chemicals. The two sides still maintain fundamentally different regulations on issues such as hormones, genetically modified organisms (GMOs), cosmetics, and the registration and restriction of chemical substances. U.S. and EU regulators continue to operate with starkly different regulatory philosophies and styles. And the record of transatlantic regulatory cooperation in this sphere has been highly contentious, prompting the United States to file a legal complaint with the WTO.[52]
5. There has been lack of material progress in many other sectors, such as autos, and pharmaceuticals. Moreover, past TRC initiatives have

tended to be fragmented, poorly coordinated, and lacking in political accountability for success and failure.[53]

Obstacles and Options for More Extensive Cooperation

In evaluating the history of past initiatives, a number of observers have pointed to several key obstacles to more effective regulatory cooperation. High on this list are the independence of regulatory agencies involved, the lack of committed resources for transatlantic regulatory collaboration, and the sheer complexity of the undertaking. To promote more effective TRC by overcoming these obstacles, three policy options are often put forth: (1) attracting high-level political support for TRC; (2) increasing dramatically the involvement of legislators on both sides in the process; and (3) developing an institutional architecture that can prioritize the problems and challenges that need to be addressed.

Regulatory cooperation, particularly mutual recognition, requires domestic regulators to accept the competency of their foreign counterparts to conduct product testing. A key obstacle, however, is that regulators remain accountable to domestic legislators for the product standards that are applied both to domestic and foreign products. As a result, regulators on both sides of the Atlantic are generally reluctant to transfer authority to a foreign body, and the MRA negotiations demonstrated that some regulatory bodies are more reluctant than others.[54]

Based on the premise that enhanced regulatory cooperation, particularly through mutual recognition, will never happen if matters are left to individual regulatory agencies, high-level political pressure is commonly prescribed. Such pressure, either from the White House, the Congress, or both, may be employed to convince regulators to adopt reforms that result in a reduction of barriers between the United States and EU and/or to make greater efforts to accommodate transatlantic interests when promulgating new regulations.

Successful regulatory cooperation also requires resources for the necessary meetings and dialogues to take place. At least on the U.S. side, the regulatory agencies have no dedicated budgets to support these activities. Accordingly, some stakeholders, such as the U.S. Chamber of Commerce, have proposed that Congress consider the creation of specifically funded mandates to enable U.S. agencies better participate in these transatlantic dialogues.

The scope of the transatlantic regulatory agenda is also extremely broad and technical. Encompassing most regulatory agencies, ranging from the Food and Drug Administration (FDA) and the Consumer Product Safety Commission (CPSC) to the National Highway Traffic Safety Administration (NHTSA) and the Environmental Protection Agency (EPA), and diverse sectors, ranging from pharmaceuticals and cosmetics to telecommunications and marine safety, the status of the agenda at any one time is not easy to ascertain. To move issues forward that are by their nature abstract and technical, some observers have called for creation of a institution that is capable of setting priorities and deciding on which issues are ripe for resolution with the help of higher-level political intervention.

THE TRANSATLANTIC ECONOMIC COUNCIL

Predicated on the notion that past initiatives failed to make significant progress in enhancing regulatory progress, the Transatlantic Economic Council (TEC) was established in April 2007 at the U.S.-EU Summit as a key component of the *Framework for Advancing Transatlantic Economic Integration.* Created as a new entity by German Chancellor Angela Merkel (then EU Council President), European Commission President Barroso, and President Bush, the TEC is designed to provide minister-level political guidance for implementation of a work program as outlined by the *Framework* to foster regulatory cooperation and to reduce or eliminate regulatory burdens to trade. The Summit leaders also created an advisory group to the TEC and invited the U.S. Congress, along with the European Parliament, to accept a new, more substantive role in transatlantic regulatory cooperation by becoming part of an advisory group. In short, the TEC and the *Framework* are designed to deal with some of the suggested shortcomings (described above) of previous transatlantic regulatory initiatives: lack of high level political leadership and not enough involvement of legislators and other stakeholders in the regulatory process.

The TEC consists of two co-chairs (ministerial-level appointees with cabinet rank) from each side, as well as a number of EU Commissioners and U.S. Cabinet members for the broad-ranging policy areas covered in the *Framework.* Permanent members of the TEC include the Secretaries of the Treasury and Commerce and the U.S. Trade Representative and the European Commissioners for External Relations, for Trade and Internal Market and

Services. In addition, other U.S. Cabinet members and European Commissioners may participate when the agenda covers issues falling under their jurisdiction.[55]

Given that the two TEC leaders are cabinet-level appointees, the TEC was expected to have the kind of high-level political support that previous efforts at economic integration may have lacked. Such clout, it is argued, may be needed to persuade domestic regulators to yield some of their authorities or to better cooperate with their counterparts across the Atlantic in harmonizing regulatory approaches.[56]

TEC efforts to foster cooperation and reduce regulatory barriers focus on two main types of issues: (1) differences in regulatory processes and approaches; and (2) sectoral or bilateral barriers and disputes. The goal in the first issue area is to find ways to reduce barriers to transatlantic economic integration posed by new regulations and or prevent them from happening. The primary avenue for accomplishing this objective entails efforts to reform, harmonize or converge regulatory processes, both through the development of comparable methodologies to assess risk and do cost-benefit analysis and intensified interactions among regulators. How regulations are developed and applied can have a large impact on the how companies do business not only in the transatlantic marketplace, but in third markets as well.

The goal in the second issue area is to reduce barriers to transatlantic integration caused by regulations in specific sectors. This is to be accomplished by intensified sector-by-sector cooperation, including the promotion of the 2002 U.S.-EU Guidelines for Regulatory Cooperation and case-by-case examination of specific projects called for by the Roadmap for Regulatory Cooperation.[57]

In the first three years (2007-2009) of its five-year history, the TEC was used primarily as a mechanism to try to resolve a number of longstanding bilateral trade disputes, most notably the EU's ban on imports of chlorine-washed poultry. Efforts to harmonize regulations on a sector-by- sector basis also proved difficult due to political and bureaucratic resistance on both sides to revise existing laws and regulations. In late 2010, the two sides agreed to focus future efforts on aligning regulations and standards in emerging or new technologies, (such as nanotechnology or electric cars) well before laws or regulations have been promulgated. Accordingly, at their fifth recent meeting, held in Washington on December 17, 2010, the TEC agreed to a work program focusing on sectors where regulatory cooperation can help preclude unintended trade barriers.

Among the highlights of this TEC meeting, the two sides agreed to develop a process to implement compatible approaches for the regulation of new and innovative sectors, with the hope of avoiding trade disputes due to different regulations. The meeting also provided new impetus for regulatory cooperation in specific sectors such as electronic health records, energy-saving products, and electric vehicles, as a way of reducing costs and preempting unnecessary obstacles to exports. Finally, the TEC meeting launched an Innovation Action Plan designed to strengthen joint efforts to promote innovation and the commercialization of emerging technologies.[58]

At its sixth meeting held in November 2011, TEC leaders reviewed accomplishments in 2011 and established priorities for 2012. Among the accomplishments, the TEC noted a number of steps taken to develop a transatlantic market for electric vehicles and endorsed a work plan for e-mobility, electric vehicles, and related infrastructure. As in many other areas supported by the TEC, it remains to be seen whether the results will prove tangible and commercially significant. This is due, in part, to the fact that regulatory cooperation is difficult and technically demanding work, with wide differences between the two sides concerning approaches to regulation.[59]

ROLE OF CONGRESS[60]

Since it began nearly two decades ago, transatlantic regulatory cooperation has been for the most part a wholly run undertaking between the executive branches and independent regulatory agencies on both sides of the Atlantic. By and large, TRC exchanges and dialogues have been confined to regulators and officials of the executive branches on both sides of the Atlantic. The *Guidelines on Regulatory Cooperation and Transparency*, in fact, do not apply to Congress or the European Parliament.

The role of Congress in transatlantic regulatory cooperation in the past has been limited mostly to oversight hearings (see **Appendix A** for a listing) and the introduction of a few resolutions.[61] But Congress has on occasion taken actions that have both thwarted and facilitated regulatory cooperation. For example, on the one hand, some Members of Congress became concerned in the late 1990s that the MRAs the administration was negotiating could harm consumers and undermine health and safety standards. As Representative Henry Waxman (D-CA) put it, "there is no question that international agreements of this kind can enhance the efficiency of commerce, but it is equally clear that they can potentially depress American health and safety standards." According to one observer, such concerns made some U.S. regulators reluctant to participate in the MRA negotiations.[62]

On the other hand, Congress also passed legislation directing the FDA to support efforts of the Department of Commerce and USTR to implement MRAs. In the Food and Drug Administration Modernization Act of 1997 (P.L. 105-115), a bill to speed the FDA approval process for new drugs and medical devices, a provision directed the FDA to support the efforts of Commerce and the Office of the U.S. Trade Representative to implement MRAs. According to the same observer, inclusion of the MRA language in the legislation was an important step toward finishing the agreement.[63]

These examples highlight a larger and more pivotal role Congress could play in regulatory cooperation if it chose to become more involved. To the extent that an overwhelming domestic orientation of regulatory agencies is a problem in moving TRC initiatives forward, Congress has the power through both the authorization and appropriations process to mandate that U.S. regulators cooperate. Congress can also ensure that the U.S. agencies involved in regulatory cooperation have the necessary budgetary and organizational resources to get the job done. Conversely, if Congress views transatlantic initiatives as moving too far in the direction of trade expansion at the expense of safety and health concerns or other priorities, Congress can make it difficult for U.S. agencies to continue on that course of action.

Beyond providing guidance to U.S. regulatory agencies on TRC initiatives, Congress also could play a bigger role in preventing new legislation from causing new transatlantic regulatory barriers. Currently, taking the transatlantic impact (trade and investment effects) into account is not considered in any structured or formal fashion during the legislative process. Yet, political declarations from past U.S.-EU summits backed by the transatlantic business community, have urged a more institutionalized process for making Congress more aware of the potential impact of new legislation on transatlantic trade.

How this could be done is the subject of considerable speculation. One of the factors that has to be considered is the wide range of congressional committees that have primary jurisdiction over issues that are high on the agenda of TRC. As shown in **Appendix B**, many different authorizing committees have primary jurisdiction over some of the main regulatory agencies involved in TRC activities. On the House side, the Energy and

Commerce, Transportation, Judiciary, and Agriculture Committees all have important oversight roles. Counterpart committees on the Senate side include Commerce, Science, and Transportation, Health Education, Labor, and Pensions, Energy and Natural Resources, Environment and Public Works, and Agriculture. Notably absent from this list are the committees charged with overall responsibility for oversight of transatlantic relations, the Senate Foreign Relations and the House Foreign Affairs Committees, and the committees that have primary jurisdiction over trade and investment issues, Senate Finance and the House Ways and Means.

Currently, the only formal institutional link between Congress and transatlantic regulatory cooperation is through the Transatlantic Legislators Dialogue (TLD), an inter-parliamentary exchange between selected Members of the House of Representatives and the European Parliament. The TLD serves as an advisor to the TEC, but its membership and function have raised questions concerning how well it can carry out its role as an advisor to the TEC.[64]

Much of this begs the question whether Congress should be an advisor or a participant in the TRC process, including the annual U.S.-EU Summits. While a more proactive role for Congress would likely enhance the political basis of support for transatlantic regulatory cooperation, it is by no means certain that there is a consensus in favor of developing the necessary mechanisms and mandate to move in this direction.

APPENDIX A. CONGRESSIONAL HEARINGS ON TRANSATLANTIC REGULATORY COOPERATION

House Committee on Commerce. *Imported Drugs: U.S.-EU Mutual Recognition Agreement on Drug Prescriptions*. October 2, 1998, 32p.

House Committee on Commerce. *The EU Data Protection Directive: Implications for the U.S. Privacy Debate*. March 8, 2001, 48p.

House Committee on Financial Services. *The EU's Financial Services Action Plan and Its Implications for the American Financial Services Industry*. May 22, 2002, 122p.

House Committee on Financial Services. *U.S.-EU Regulatory Dialogue and Its Future*. May 13, 2004, 106p.

House Committee on Financial Services. *U.S.-EU Regulatory Dialogue: The Private Sector Perspective*. June 17, 2004, 79p.

House Committee on Financial Services. *U.S.-EU Economic Relationship: What Comes Next*? June 16, 2005, 86p.

House Committee on International Relations. *Transatlantic Trade Agenda: Conflict or Cooperation*? September 29, 1999.

House Committee on International Relations. *Recognizing the Continued Importance of the Transatlantic Relationship and Promoting Stronger Relations with Europe by Reaffirming the Need for a Continued and Meaningful Dialogue Between the U.S. and Europe*. October 29, 2003, 16p.

Senate Committee on Foreign Relations. *U.S.-EU Cooperation on Regulatory Affairs*. October 16, 2003, 55p.

Senate Committee on Foreign Relations. *U.S.-EU Regulatory Cooperation on Emerging Technologies*, May 11, 2005, 62p.

APPENDIX B. U.S.-EU REGULATORY COOPERATION BY SECTOR, U.S. REGULATORY AGENCY, AND COMMITTEE OVERSIGHT

Sector[a]	U.S. Regulatory Agency[b]	Committees[c]
Pharmaceuticals	Food and Drug Administration (FDA)	House: Energy and Commerce; Senate: Health, Education, Labor, and Pensions and Commerce Science and Transportation
Automobile Safety	National Highway Traffic Safety Administration (NHTSA)	House: Energy and Commerce; Senate: Commerce, Science and Transportation
Information and Communications Standards in Regulations	Department of Commerce, National Institute of Standards and Technology (NIST)	House: Energy and Commerce; Senate: Commerce, Science and Transportation
Cosmetics	FDA	House: Energy and Commerce; Senate: Health, Education, Labor, and Pensions
Consumer Product Safety	Consumer Product Safety Commission (CPSC)	House: Energy and Commerce; Senate: Commerce, Science, and Transportation
Consumer Protection Enforcement Cooperation	Federal Trade Commission (FTC)	House: Energy and Commerce, and Judiciary; Senate: Commerce, Science and Transportation, and Judiciary

Sector[a]	U.S. Regulatory Agency[b]	Committees[c]
Unfair Commercial Practices	FTC	House: Energy and Commerce, and Judiciary;
		Senate: Commerce, Science, and Transportation, and Judiciary
Nutritional Labeling	FDA	House: Energy and Commerce, and Agriculture;
		Senate: Heath, Education, Labor and Pensions, and Agriculture
Food Safety	FDA	House: Energy and Commerce Agriculture;
		Senate: Commerce, Science, and Transportation, and Agriculture
Marine Equipment	U.S. Coast Guard	House: Transportation and Infrastructure;
		Senate: Commerce, Science, and Transportation
Eco-Design	Environmental Protection Agency (EPA); Department of Energy Office of Efficiency and Renewable Energy	House: Energy and Commerce an Science;
		Senate: Energy and Natural Resources
Chemicals	Environmental Protection Agency	House: Energy and Commerce ;
		Senate: Environment and Public Works
Energy Efficiency	EPA and Department of Energy	House: Energy and Commerce
		Senate: Energy and Natural Resources
Medical Devices	FDA	House: Energy and Commerce;
		Senate:
Telecommunications and Radio Communications Equipment	Federal Communications Commission and Department of Commerce, National Institute of Standards and Technology	House: Energy and Commerce ;
		Senate: Commerce, Science, and Transportation

Source: CRS.

[a] These sectors are identified in the 2005 *Roadmap for Regulatory Cooperation*, http://www.ustr.gov?World_Regions/Europe_Middle_East/Europe/US_EU-Regulatory-C.

[b] These agencies are also identified in the 2005 *Roadmap for Regulatory Cooperation*.

[c] Depending on the focus of each sectoral initiative, other committees could also have oversight responsibilities. Regarding appropriations, the appropriations subcommittees would tend to vary as well. For example, the House and Senate Appropriations subcommittees on agriculture have jurisdiction over FDA's appropriations. This arrangement reflects, in part, the agency's origin within the Department of Agriculture as the Bureau of Chemistry in 1862.

End Notes

[1] For background on the European Union, see CRS Report RS21372, *The European Union: Questions and Answers*, by Kristin Archick and Derek E. Mix.

[2] For background on EU-U.S. commercial ties, see CRS Report RL30608, *EU-U.S. Economic Ties: Framework, Scope, and Magnitude*, by William H. Cooper; and CRS Report R41652, *U.S.-EU Trade and Economic Relations: Key Policy Issues for the 112th Congress*, by Raymond J. Ahearn.

[3] The NTA committed the United States and EU to work together to achieve four major goals, including the expansion of world trade and closer economic relations. Implementation of the agenda is guided by a joint EU-U.S. Action Plan which is coordinated by a group of senior level officials.

[4] For background on the 2007 U.S.-EU Summit and the TEC, see http://www.whitehouse.gov/infocus/eusummit/2007/.

[5] Daniel C. Esty, "Regulatory Competition in Focus," *Journal of International Economic Law* (2000), pp. 215-217.

[6] Reinhard Quick, "Transatlantic Regulatory Cooperation on Chemicals—An Idealist's Dream?," German Marshall Fund Academic Research Conference, Ford School, University of Michigan. Available at http://www.fordschool.umich.edu/news/events_details/re_coop_and-comp_08/, and Gregory C. Shaffer and Mark A. Pollack, "Reconciling Regulatory Differences: The Ongoing Transatlantic Dispute over the Regulation of Biotechnology," in *The Future of Transatlantic Economic Relations,* edited by David M. Andrews, Mark A. Pollack, Gregory C. Shaffer, and Helen Wallace, Robert Schuman Centre for Advanced Studies, 2005, pp. 220-221.

[7] Keith Maskus and Yin He, "Trans-Atlantic Regulatory Cooperation in Pharmaceuticals: An Intellectual Property and Trade Perspective," German Marshall Fund Academic Policy Research Conference, May 8-9, 2008, Ford School, University of Michigan, p. 8. Available at http://www.fordschool.umich.edu/news/events_details/ reg_coop_and_comp_08/.

[8] Vann H. Wilber and Paul T. Eichbrecht, "Transatlantic Trade, the Automotive Sector: The Role of Regulation in a Global Industry, Where We Have Been and Where We Need To Go, How Far Can EU-US Cooperation Go Toward Achieving Regulatory Harmonization," German Marshall Fund Academic Policy Research Conference, Ford School, University of Michigan, p. 7. Available at http://fordschool.umich.edu/news/events_details/re_coop_and_comp_08/.

[9] Office of the U.S. Trade Representative, 2008 National Trade Estimate Report on Foreign Trade Barriers, pp. 9-21. Available at http://www.ustr.gov.

[10] David Vogel, "Can it be done? Suggestions for better regulatory cooperation between the US and Europe," Transatlantic Thinkers #7, Bertelsmann Stiftung, p. 3. Available at http://www.bertelsmann-stiftung.de/cps/rde/xchg/ bst_engl/hs.xsl/prj_7072-7084.htm.

[11] Vann H. Wilber and Paul T. Eichbrecht, "Transatlantic Trade, the Automotive Sector: The Role of Regulation in a Global Industry, Where We Have Been and Where We Need To Go, How Far Can EU-US Cooperation Go Toward Achieving Regulatory Harmonization," German Marshall Fund Academic Policy Research Conference, May 8-9, 2008, p. 5. Available at http://fordschool.umich.edu/news/events_details/re_coop_andcomp_08/.

[12] OECD Working Paper No. 432, *On the Benefits of Liberalizing Product Markets and Reducing Barriers to International Trade and Investment: The Case of the United States and European Union* May 26, 2005.

[13] The initial impetus for promoting a transatlantic dialogue on regulatory standards was the European Community's 1992 internal market program. At the heart of this program was an effort to establish European-wide standards. Progress along these lines raised concerns in the U.S. business community that the new standards and regulations could be used to disadvantage U.S. exporters and products.

[14] Daniel C. Esty and Damien Geradin, "Regulatory Co-opetition," *Journal of International Economic Law* (2000), 235-255, p. 236.

[15] Transatlantic Policy Network (TPN), *Completing the Transatlantic Market,* February 2007, pp. 6-7. Available at http://tpnonline.org.

[16] Simon J. Everett and Robert M. Stern, "Condemned To Cooperate?," German Marshall Fund Academic Policy Research Conference, May 8-9, 2008, University of Michigan, p. 7. Available at http://www.fordschool.umich.edu/ news/events_details/re_coop_08/.

[17] Gregory Shaffer and Mark Pollack, "How Hard and Soft Law Interact in International Regulatory Governance: Alternatives, Complements or Antagonists?," German Marshall Fund Academic Policy Research Conference, May 8-9, 2008. University of Michigan, p. 5. Available at http://www.fordschool.umich.edu/news/events_details/reg_coop_andcomp_08.

[18] Reinhard Quick, "Regulatory Cooperation—A Subject of Bilateral Trade Negotiations or Even for the WTO?," *Journal of World Trade Law* 42(3), 2008, p. 405.

[19] David Vogel, op. cit., p. 4.

[20] Ibid., p. 5.

[21] Trans-Atlantic Consumer Dialogue, "Position Paper and Resolution on Horizontal Regulatory Initiatives in EU-U.S. Regulatory Cooperation," February 2007. Available at http://www.tacd.org/cgi-bin/db.cgi?page=view&config=admin/docs.cfg&id=322.

[22] Reinhard Quick, op. cit., p. 401.

[23] David Vogel, op. cit., p. 14.

[24] Ibid., p. 7.

[25] At the same time, in 1980s and throughout much of the 1990s, much of U.S. policy was driven by efforts to reduce the costs of protective regulations on American companies and, thus, improve the performance of the American economy.

[26] Jackie Calmes, "Both Sides of the Aisle See More Regulation," *New York Times,* October 14, 2008, p. 1.

[27] David Vogel, op. cit., p. 6.

[28] Gregory C. Shaffer and Mark A. Pollack, op. cit., p. 221.

[29] Testimony of Gerard Depayre, Deputy Head of Delegation, European Commission to the United States, "U.S.-EU Cooperation on Regulatory Affairs," Hearing Before the Subcommittee on European Affairs of the Committee on Foreign Relations, U.S. Senate, 108th Congress, 1st session, October 16, 2003, p. 20.

[30] Kalypso Nicolaidis and Rebecca Steffenson, "Managed Mutual Recognition in the Transatlantic Marketplace," in *The Future of Transatlantic Economic Relations,* p. 147.

[31] Maria Green Cowles, "Calming the Waters: The Rebirth of the Transatlantic Business Dialogue," in *The Future of Transatlantic Economic Relations,* p. 285.

[32] Kalypso Nicolaidis and Rebecca Steffenson, p. 152.

[33] Alan O. Sykes, "Regulatory Competition or Regulatory Harmonisation? A Silly Question?," *Journal of International Economic Law* (2000), pp. 257-264.

[34] Reinhard Quick, "Regulatory Cooperation," op. cit., p. 402.

[35] Testimony of Stuart Eizenstat, European-American Business Council, Hearing on U.S.-EU Cooperation on Regulatory Affairs, Subcommittee on European Affairs of the Committee on Foreign Relations, U.S. Senate, 108th Congress, 1st session, October 16, 2003, p. 29.

[36] Charan Devereaux, Robert Z. Lawrence, and Michael D. Watkins, "The U.S.-EU Mutual Recognition Agreements," in *Case Studies in US Trade Negotiations,* in Making the Rules, Vol. 1, Institute for International Economics, 2006, p. 304.

[37] Stuart Eisenstadt, op. cit., p. 24.

[38] The U.S. Chamber of Commerce, for example, has proposed an Agreement on Regulatory Cooperation (ARC), a legally binding regulatory cooperation agreement that would oblige both sides to operate under a common set of regulatory principles and core beliefs. The ARC would require regulators to assess the cost impact of forthcoming regulations on transatlantic commerce, adopt other's best practices where possible, and utilize a similar

methodology to assess costs and benefits of proposed regulations. See Chamber of Commerce of the United States, Correspondence to U.S. Office of Management and Budget and to the Secretariat General, European Commission, February 8, 2008.

[39] Reinhard Quick, "Regulatory Cooperation," p. 401.

[40] Ibid.

[41] The Atlantic Council of the United States, *Risk and Reward: U.S.-EU Regulatory Cooperation on Food Safety and the Environment,* Policy Paper, November 2002, p. 7.

[42] Maria Green Cowles, "Calming the Waters: The Rebirth of the Transatlantic Business Dialogue," p. 278.

[43] Robert Anderson, "Competition (Antitrust) Policy: What Balance of Cooperation and Regulation in the Transatlantic Sphere?," German Marshall Fund Academic Policy Research Conference, May 8-9, 2008, Ford School, University of Michigan, p. 5. Available at http://www.fordschool.umich.edu/news/events_details/reg_coop_and_comp_08/.

[44] Maria Green Cowles, "Calming the Waters: The Rebirth of the Transatlantic Business Dialogue," p. 280.

[45] Charon Devereaux, Robert Z. Lawrence, and Michael D. Watkins, "The U.S.-EU Mutual Recognition Agreements," p. 348.

[46] Elliott Posner, "Market Power without a Single Market: The New Transatlantic Relations in Financial Services," In *The Future of Transatlantic Economic Relations: Continuity Amid Discord,* July 2005.

[47] Andreas Noelke, Johan Wolfgang Goethe Universitat, "Transatlantic Regulatory Cooperation on Accounting Standards: A 'Varieties of Capitalism' Perspective," German Marshall Fund Academic Policy Research Conference, May 8-9, 2008, Ford School, University of Michigan. Available at http://fordschool.umich.edu/news/events_details_/reg_cop_and_comp_08/.

[48] Kalypso Nicolaidis and Rebecca Steffenson, "Managed Mutual Recognition in the Transatlantic Marketplace," p. 148.

[49] Gregory Shaffer, "Managing U.S.-EU Trade Relations Through Mutual Recognition and Safe Harbor Agreements: 'New' and 'Global' Approaches to Transatlantic Economic Governance?", 9 *Columbia Journal of European Law,* 29- 77 (Fall 2002), p. 43.

[50] Stuart Eizenstad, op. cit. p. 26.

[51] Reinhardt Quick, "Regulatory Cooperation," p. 399.

[52] Reinhardt Quick, "Transatlantic Regulatory Cooperation on Chemicals—An Idealist's Dream?," German Marshall Fund Academic Policy Research Conference, May 8-9, 2008, Ford School, University of Michigan. Available at http://fordschool.umch.edu/nes/events_details/reg_coop_and_comp_08/.

[53] Testimony of Kathryn Hauser, U.S. Executive Director of the Transatlantic Business Dialogue, House Committee on Financial Services, "The U.S.-EU Economic Relationship: What Comes Next?," June 16, 2005, p. 9.

[54] Kalypso Nicolaidais and Rebecca Steffenson, p. 145.

[55] To co-chair the TEC, the Obama Administration appointed Michael Froman, Deputy National Security Advisor for International Economic Affairs, National Economic Council. The EU co-chair is the EU Trade Commissioner, Karel De Gucht.

[56] For more information on the TEC, see Section IV in the U.S.-EU Framework for Advancing Transatlantic Economic Integration, April 2007, available at http://www.whitehouse.gov/releases/2007/04/20070430-4.html.

[57] The Regulatory Cooperation Roadmap provides a framework of dialogues in 15 different sectors, including pharmaceuticals, telecommunications equipment, food safety, and auto safety.

[58] International Trade Reporter, "Transatlantic Council Meeting Advances Regulatory Cooperation, Innovative Strategies," 27 ITR 1963, December 23, 2010.

[59] See CRS Report RL34717, *Transatlantic Regulatory Cooperation: Background and Analysis*, pp. 7-9.

[60] For additional information, CRS Report RL34735, *Transatlantic Regulatory Cooperation: A Possible Role for Congress*, by Raymond J. Ahearn and Vincent Morelli.

[61] In December 2006, the Senate passed a resolution (S.Res. 632) calling for the completion of the Transatlantic Market by 2015. The resolution also called for a jointly funded, cooperatively led study of existing barriers to transatlantic trade and investment, including sector-by-sector estimates of the costs and benefits of removing such obstacles and a timetable for their removal.

[62] Congressman Henry Waxman, Hearing before the House Subcommittee on Oversight and Investigations of the Committee on Commerce, "Imported Drugs: U.S.-EU Mutual Recognition Agreement on Drug Prescriptions," 105th Congress, 2nd session, October 2, 1998, p. 4.

[63] Charan Devereaux, Robert Z. Lawrence, and Michael D. Watkins, "The U.S.-EU Mutual Recognition Agreements," p. 339.

[64] The TLD as currently structured does not include members of the Senate on the U.S. side. For more information on the role of the TLD, see pp. 10-16 of CRS Report RL34735, *Transatlantic Regulatory Cooperation: A Possible Role for Congress*, by Raymond J. Ahearn and Vincent Morelli.

In: International Regulatory Cooperation
Editor: Lenore Lynch
ISBN: 978-1-63117-276-2

Chapter 3

EXECUTIVE ORDER 13609 – PROMOTING INTERNATIONAL REGULATORY COOPERATION*

Barack Obama

By the authority vested in me as President by the Constitution and the laws of the United States of America, and in order to promote international regulatory cooperation, it is hereby ordered as follows:

Section 1. Policy. Executive Order 13563 of January 18, 2011 (Improving Regulation and Regulatory Review), states that our regulatory system must protect public health, welfare, safety, and our environment while promoting economic growth, innovation, competitiveness, and job creation. In an increasingly global economy, international regulatory cooperation, consistent with domestic law and prerogatives and U.S. trade policy, can be an important means of promoting the goals of Executive Order 13563.

The regulatory approaches taken by foreign governments may differ from those taken by U.S. regulatory agencies to address similar issues. In some cases, the differences between the regulatory approaches of U.S. agencies and those of their foreign counterparts might not be necessary and might impair the ability of American businesses to export and compete internationally. In meeting shared challenges involving health, safety, labor, security, environmental, and other issues, international regulatory cooperation can

* This Executive Order was submitted by the White House May 1, 2012.

identify approaches that are at least as protective as those that are or would be adopted in the absence of such cooperation. International regulatory cooperation can also reduce, eliminate, or prevent unnecessary differences in regulatory requirements.

Sec. 2. Coordination of International Regulatory Cooperation. (a) The Regulatory Working Group (Working Group) established by Executive Order 12866 of September 30, 1993 (Regulatory Planning and Review), which was reaffirmed by Executive Order 13563, shall, as appropriate:

(i) serve as a forum to discuss, coordinate, and develop a common understanding among agencies of U.S. Government positions and priorities with respect to:

(A) international regulatory cooperation activities that are reasonably anticipated to lead to significant regulatory actions;
(B) efforts across the Federal Government to support significant, cross-cutting international regulatory cooperation activities, such as the work of regulatory cooperation councils; and
(C) the promotion of good regulatory practices internationally, as well as the promotion of U.S. regulatory approaches, as appropriate; and

(ii) examine, among other things:

(A) appropriate strategies for engaging in the development of regulatory approaches through international regulatory cooperation, particularly in emerging technology areas, when consistent with section 1 of this order;
(B) best practices for international regulatory cooperation with respect to regulatory development, and, where appropriate, information exchange and other regulatory tools; and
(C) factors that agencies should take into account when determining whether and how to consider other regulatory approaches under section 3(d) of this order.

(b) As Chair of the Working Group, the Administrator of the Office of Information and Regulatory Affairs (OIRA) of the Office of Management and Budget (OMB) shall convene the Working Group as necessary to discuss international regulatory cooperation issues as described above, and the Working Group shall include a representative from the Office of the United States Trade

Representative and, as appropriate, representatives from other agencies and offices.

(c) The activities of the Working Group, consistent with law, shall not duplicate the efforts of existing interagency bodies and coordination mechanisms. The Working Group shall consult with existing interagency bodies when appropriate.

(d) To inform its discussions, and pursuant to section 4 of Executive Order 12866, the Working Group may commission analytical reports and studies by OIRA, the Administrative Conference of the United States, or any other relevant agency, and the Administrator of OIRA may solicit input, from time to time, from representatives of business, nongovernmental organizations, and the public.

(e) The Working Group shall develop and issue guidelines on the applicability and implementation of sections 2 through 4 of this order.

(f) For purposes of this order, the Working Group shall operate by consensus.

Sec. 3. Responsibilities of Federal Agencies. To the extent permitted by law, and consistent with the principles and requirements of Executive Order 13563 and Executive Order 12866, each agency shall:

(a) if required to submit a Regulatory Plan pursuant to Executive Order 12866, include in that plan a summary of its international regulatory cooperation activities that are reasonably anticipated to lead to significant regulations, with an explanation of how these activities advance the purposes of Executive Order 13563 and this order;

(b) ensure that significant regulations that the agency identifies as having significant international impacts are designated as such in the Unified Agenda of Federal Regulatory and Deregulatory Actions, on RegInfo.gov, and on Regulations.gov;

(c) in selecting which regulations to include in its retrospective review plan, as required by Executive Order 13563, consider:

(i) reforms to existing significant regulations that address unnecessary differences in regulatory requirements between the United States and its major trading partners, consistent with section 1 of this order, when stakeholders provide adequate information to the agency establishing that the differences are unnecessary; and

(ii) such reforms in other circumstances as the agency deems appropriate; and

(d) for significant regulations that the agency identifies as having significant international impacts, consider, to the extent feasible, appropriate, and consistent with law, any regulatory approaches by a foreign government that the United States has agreed to consider under a regulatory cooperation council work plan.

Sec. 4. Definitions. For purposes of this order:

(a) "Agency" means any authority of the United States that is an "agency" under 44 U.S.C. 3502(1), other than those considered to be independent regulatory agencies, as defined in 44 U.S.C. 3502(5).
(b) "International impact" is a direct effect that a proposed or final regulation is expected to have on international trade and investment, or that otherwise may be of significant interest to the trading partners of the United States.
(c) "International regulatory cooperation" refers to a bilateral, regional, or multilateral process, other than processes that are covered by section 6(a)(ii), (iii), and (v) of this order, in which national governments engage in various forms of collaboration and communication with respect to regulations, in particular a process that is reasonably anticipated to lead to the development of significant regulations.
(d) "Regulation" shall have the same meaning as "regulation" or "rule" in section 3(d) of Executive Order 12866.
(e) "Significant regulation" is a proposed or final regulation that constitutes a significant regulatory action.
(f) "Significant regulatory action" shall have the same meaning as in section 3(f) of Executive Order 12866.

Sec. 5. Independent Agencies. Independent regulatory agencies are encouraged to comply with the provisions of this order.

Sec. 6. General Provisions. (a) Nothing in this order shall be construed to impair or otherwise affect:

i. the authority granted by law to a department or agency, or the head thereof;
ii. the coordination and development of international trade policy and negotiations pursuant to section 411 of the Trade Agreements Act of 1979 (19 U.S.C. 2451) and section 141 of the Trade Act of 1974 (19 U.S.C. 2171);

iii. international trade activities undertaken pursuant to section 3 of the Act of February 14, 1903 (15 U.S.C. 1512), subtitle C of the Export Enhancement Act of 1988, as amended (15 U.S.C. 4721 et seq.), and Reorganization Plan No. 3 of 1979 (19 U.S.C. 2171 note);
iv. the authorization process for the negotiation and conclusion of international agreements pursuant to 1 U.S.C. 112b(c) and its implementing regulations (22 C.F.R. 181.4) and implementing procedures (11 FAM 720);
v. activities in connection with subchapter II of chapter 53 of title 31 of the United States Code, title 26 of the United States Code, or Public Law 111–203 and other laws relating to financial regulation; or
vi. the functions of the Director of OMB relating to budgetary, administrative, or legislative proposals.

(b) This order shall be implemented consistent with applicable law and subject to the availability of appropriations.

(c) This order is not intended to, and does not, create any right or benefit, substantive or procedural, enforceable at law or in equity by any party against the United States, its departments, agencies, or entities, its officers, employees, or agents, or any other person.

Barack Obama

INDEX

A

B

C

D

E

F

G

H

I

J

K

L